SOFT SKILLS FOR TOUGH COOKIES

HOW TO DEAL WITH DIFFICULT MANAGERS

 FriesenPress

Suite 300 - 990 Fort St
Victoria, BC, V8V 3K2
Canada

www.friesenpress.com

ISBN
978-1-5255-4063-9 (Hardcover)
978-1-5255-4064-6 (Paperback)
978-1-5255-4065-3 (eBook)

1. BUSINESS & ECONOMICS, HUMAN RESOURCES & PERSONNEL MANAGEMENT

Distributed to the trade by The Ingram Book Company

Table of Contents

Introduction 1

Chapter 1: What is a Tough Cookie? 3

    Personality Conflicts 4

    I-am-right William 5

Chapter 2: What Makes a Tough Cookie, Tough? 7

    Learning 7

    Low Self-Monitoring 8

    The Stress Response and the Fatal Flaw 9

Chapter 3: The Making of a Tough Cookie 11

    I was a Tough Cookie 11

    How Do You Know if You're a Tough Cookie? 13

Chapter 4: The Cookies 15

    1. The Ginger Snap 16

    2. The Black and White Cookie 18

    3 The Hermit Cookie 20

    4. The Oatmeal Raisin Cookie 22

    5. The Fortune Cookie 24

    6. The Imperial Cookie 26

    7. The Refrigerator Cookie 28

    8. The Shortbread Cookie 30

    9. The Double Chocolate Macadamia Nut Cookie (DCCMN) ... 32

    10. The Chocolate Puff Cookie 34

    11. The Sugar Cookie 36

12. Cookie Dough 38

Summary 39

Chapter 5: So, I am Tough Cookie. Now What? 41

Why Soft Skills? 41

Personality Change is Not Required 42

Tough Cookies have Great Strengths 44

Chapter 6: Strategies to Get You Started 45

First Steps for Tough Cookies 45

Notice How You Communicate 46

Notice How Others Communicate 46

Notice Your Impact on Others 47

The Mirror Exercise 48

Part A: Self-reflection 48

Part B: Self-analysis 48

Part C: Self-analysis 49

Start Small, People Get Suspicious 49

Recognize the Absence of Trust 50

Overlearn New Skills 52

First Steps if You are Working with a Practising Cookie 52

The Feedback Dilemma 53

Corrective Feedback 53

The Going Forward Dilemma 53

Chapter 7: The Ginger Snap 55

Summary of Strengths and Challenges 55

The Story of Bob 56

Strategies for the Ginger Snap. 57

Strategies for Being Less Snappy 58

If You Are Working With a Ginger Snap 61

Chapter 8: The Black and White Cookie 63

Summary of Strengths and Challenges 63

The World According to Alex 65

Strategies for Black and White Cookies 66

If You Are Working With a Black and White Cookie 69

Chapter 9: The Hermit Cookie 71

Summary of Strengths and Challenges... 71

"Hello? Where are you, Patrick?" 72

The Not-so-Open-Door Della 75

Strategies for Hermit Cookies 75

If You Are Working With or Know a Hermit Cookie 78

Chapter 10: The Oatmeal Raisin Cookie 79

Summary of Strengths and Challenges... 79

The Story of Dug-in Don 81

Strategies for Oatmeal Raisin Cookies.. 82

If You Are Working With or Know an Oatmeal Raisin Cookie............. 83

Chapter 11: The Fortune Cookie.. 85

Summary of Strengths and Challenges... 85

Fortune Cookie Scenario.. 86

"I'm Forced to Be Here" Sandy 88

Strategies for Fortune Cookies... 90

If You Are Working With or Know a Fortune Cookie.......................... 91

Chapter 12: The Imperial Cookie 93

Summary of Strengths and Challenges... 93

The Reign of Robert... 96

Strategies for the Imperial Cookie 98

If You Are Working With or Know an Imperial Cookie 99

Chapter 13: The Refrigerator Cookie 101

Summary of Strengths and Challenges....................................... 101

A Tale of Two Cookies and the Missing Ingredient 102

Strategies for the Refrigerator Cookie 106

If You Are Working With or Know a Refrigerator Cookie................. 107

Chapter 14: The Shortbread Cookie 109

Summary of Strengths and Challenges....................................... 109

How to Ruin a Company in a Year or Less.................................... 111

Cut the Fat, Kill the Cookie 113

Strategies for the Shortbread Tough Cookie 114

If You Are Working for a Shortbread Company or Individual............ 116

Chapter 15: The Double Chocolate Chunk Macadamia Nut Cookie 117

Summary of Strengths and Challenges 117

Strategies for the DCCMN 119

If You Are Working With or Know a DCCMN 120

Chapter 16: The Chocolate Puff 121

A Summary of Strengths and Challenges 121

The Art of Eating a Chocolate Puff 122

The Chocolate Puff Cookie 123

It was Paul and Paulette 124

If you are a Chocolate Puff 126

If You Are Working With or Know a Chocolate Puff 126

Chapter 17: The Sugar Cookie 129

Summary of Strengths and Challenges 129

Being Burnt: The Point of No Return 133

If you are a Sugar Cookie 134

If You Are Working With or Know a Sugar Cookie 135

Chapter 18: Cookie Dough 137

Summary of Strengths and Challenges 137

The Amazing Coincidence 137

The Rise to Leadership for Cookie Dough 140

The Struggle of Maury and the Missing Baking Powder 141

Directive Ain't Mean 143

If You are Cookie Dough 144

If You Work with or Know a Cookie Dough 145

Chapter 19 – Number 13 is a Monster 147

The Monster Cookie and the Riddle of a Baker's Dozen 148

The Canadian Smartie 148

Before It's Too Late 149

Chapter 20: Inside the Cookie Jar: Cookie Interactions 153

The Reality of Tough Cookies' Working Together 154

Creating a Cookie Team. What's it Gonna Take? 160

Chapter 21: The Report Card 165

The Cookie Dough Report 166

The Ginger Snap Report.. 167

The Refrigerator Cookie Report 169

The Hermit Cookie Report 170

The Tired Manager... 171

The Impact of Commitment.. 172

Chapter 22: Help! I Have Tough Cookies on My Team. 175

What Can I Expect in Tough Cookie Development? 176

Chapter 23: Cleaning up the Crumbs.. 181

The Impact.. 182

About the Author 183

Introduction

I climbed the stairs to Gerald's office. His organization had hired me as a coach to help improve his interpersonal skills, and this was our first meeting. I knocked on the door and heard a clear, "Come in." I introduced myself and sat down in the chair across the desk from him. Before I could say anything more, Gerald asked, "I'm wondering what the hell I am going to learn from you? I have over 35 years' experience!"

Not put off, I replied in a calm voice, "Well, we can talk about your family," nodding toward the pictures on his shelf, "or we can talk about why your employees are afraid of you. Either way, your company has paid for an hour of my time."

"My employees are not afraid of me and even if they were, why didn't someone tell me?" he exclaimed.

Again, calmly, I replied, "Yes, they are, and yes, you have been informed; in fact, that's why I'm here. Believe me, my being here is not a good thing. It's usually an employer's last resort."

Gerald was silent and leaned back in his chair. "I'm listening," he said.

I shared with him both the reason I was hired to coach him and what the coaching process was all about. Determined to be both frank and friendly and needing to understand his perspective, I asked questions and listened intently.

I found Gerald to be a well-intending manager and a caring individual. This, however, was not what his employer and employees saw. In order to access the friendlier side of Gerald, one had to look more closely and not be intimidated by his direct approach. This is not an easy endeavour when it's the boss that's intimidating. Gerald was a tough cookie!

Tough cookies are all too common in the workplace. It doesn't seem to matter what type of industry, there are tough cookies everywhere and some are tougher than others. They may explode unexpectedly, are resistant to change, or are so focused on the task that they forget much-needed people skills. I have found, however, that most tough cookies don't realize how they come across, don't recognize their impact on people, or haven't developed the skills to counter their tough exterior. Yet, most tough cookies want to be good managers and care about their employees. Unfortunately, getting the job done overshadows their demonstrating more relationship-oriented behaviours. Even so, I have found tough cookies aren't so tough. In fact, I have never met a tough cookie I did not like.

It turned out that Gerald became the biggest supporter of the coaching process. He developed the soft skills needed to establish rapport with employees. He succeeded—almost. It seems he forgot to apply his new skills to an interaction with his supervisor and well ... you can guess where it went from there.

How can tough cookies develop the soft skills required to be effective managers? This book will give you the skills to deal with the tough cookies and give tough cookies the skills to deal with you.

Chapter 1: What is a Tough Cookie?

People often ask me, "What type of cookie am I?"
I reply by asking, "Are you a tough cookie?"
"What's a tough cookie?" they inquire.

Here is my definition of a tough cookie:

> "Tough cookie – someone whose behaviour is extreme; does not adjust behaviour to accommodate different situations nor adjust communication style to accommodate others. Often a result of awarenessminusus and behaviourstuckedness."

The last two terms are fanciful ways of saying lack of self-awareness and lack of flexibility. I have never met a tough cookie that is not plagued by these two conditions. In fact, other people recognize tough cookies long before tough cookies are aware of their impact on others. Therefore, tough cookies find it difficult (if they find it necessary at all) to learn new skills to improve their relationship with others.

Tough cookies display distinctive behaviours that are out of sync with others or with circumstance. If guided, they may change their behaviours for the better but will often fall back into old patterns if they a) haven't overlearned the new ways of responding, and b) are not held accountable through ongoing support. People describe tough cookies as having strong personalities, which create the all-to-common personality conflict.

Personality Conflicts

In my years of working with people, I have seen many personality conflicts. Workplaces, especially, are melting pots of personalities. All organizations are made up of an assortment of people with different perspectives, backgrounds, communication styles, et cetera. For example, a person who likes to "get to the point" may conflict with someone who communicates in more detail. When this happens, people say, "It's a personality conflict!" Personality conflict is the catchall phrase used when people don't like and don't get along with each other. To a degree, it's understandable because no two people are alike. We communicate differently, and tough cookies don't communicate very well.

In conflict, we wish the other person would change. Trying to change personality is futile. We can, however, change behaviour. Tough cookies need to adjust their behaviours to work more effectively with others. This is imperative when tough cookies are in a position of authority.

Some people are better than others at adjusting their behaviours and communication styles to fit different situations. Some people are good at recognizing social cues to help them adjust. Others are seemingly clueless. The harder it is to adjust behaviour across people and circumstance, the tougher it is to communicate effectively. Tough cookies don't adjust easily, and tough cookies lack awareness. What struck me in my working with tough cookies is their lack of awareness about three things:

1. Noticing how they communicate
2. Noticing how others communicate
3. Noticing their impact on others

Some tough cookies are more willing than others to modify their behaviours. Some are more able. Most tough cookies want to do good jobs and be effective employees or managers; they just don't come across that way. They often communicate in such a way as to be not only misunderstood but also feared. People around them are frustrated. Everyone knows what the tough cookie is like, except for the tough cookie. William was a tough cookie because William was ALWAYS right.

I-am-right William

William is a very intelligent man. He took pride in his job and seemed determined to fill the role of senior supervisor effectively and efficiently. He oozed confidence. As time went on, those around him noticed the confidence begin to change to arrogance. That was the perception. That was not his intent. When William's supervisor gave him direction, William questioned it, and the amount of information he shared decreased with time. With diminishing communications and directions devolving into arguments, I was asked to work with William.

During our time together, we addressed how he was perceived. He denied being arrogant and was shocked that he would be described as such. He was also surprised to hear that he acted differently with different employees. Some he liked, and it showed. Some he did not, and it showed. We discussed favouritism and how supervisors need to focus on an employee's behaviour and not the employee. William's lack of self-awareness was impacting his performance. We worked through an example.

I asked William to play the role of an employee in conflict with a colleague. I played the role of William's supervisor. In the scenario, William requests a meeting with me. I gave William two separate responses:

In the first scenario, when William walked in, I continued to work on my computer. William explained how he was having trouble with a colleague. I interrupted him frequently and implied he might be at fault. I was subtle in my lack of support for William, but it was clear.

In the second scenario, I stopped work and greeted him. I asked questions for understanding and implied that this situation had little to do with him. Clearly, I was on William's side on this one.

At the completion of the role-play, I asked William which scenario showed I favoured him. His reply surprised me. "I don't see any difference. It was the same issue, the same colleague, and we came to the same conclusion."

I asked William if he could sense that I was treating him differently in each scenario. William replied, "No, I didn't really pay attention to any of that." He asked, "Should I have?" We spent the rest of the session discussing why the answer to that question is "yes."

In case you're a tough cookie reading this and wondering why it's important to notice such things, there is a simple answer. An effective manager needs to balance task and relationship behaviours. Task behaviours include such things as directing people, setting deadlines, or ensuring quality controls are enforced. Relationship behaviours include developing rapport, coaching, and encouraging others. In short, managers need to be technically competent social ninjas. It's a tricky balance for most, but imperative for all.

Chapter 2: What Makes a Tough Cookie, Tough?

What happens when you add too much of one ingredient when you bake cookies? They don't turn out so well. Too much ginger in a ginger snap makes it inedible. In the human-cookie world, tough cookies become tough because of a number of factors including the following:

a. Learning
b. Low self-monitoring
c. Behaviour modified by stress

Learning

In the work environment, we want to increase some behaviours and decrease others. We often do exactly the opposite. Undesirable behaviours are frequently reinforced and desirable behaviours punished. By delaying the start of meetings until everyone is present, for example, we are rewarding the chronically late and penalizing the chronically early. Tough cookie behaviours are often unknowingly solidified by those for whom the behaviours are a problem. Consider the following:

> A manager displays the undesirable quality of getting angry quickly, especially when challenged. The manager's supervisor sees this as unacceptable and says so. The challenged person becomes defensive, blames anyone and everyone for having to get angry in the first place, and then informs the supervisor that no one else has brought this to his attention. The reaction is so extreme that the supervisor is stunned into silence. Nothing is settled. The supervisor relays the incident to a senior leader who says, "Oh, that's just the way he is. Learn to ignore it." The result ... nothing is resolved. The behaviour continues. The manager has learned that people will leave him alone if he explodes.

Low Self-Monitoring

Self-monitoring is watching how one fits into accepted behaviour. If I pay close attention to my impact on you, for example, I will know when I annoy you. It doesn't mean I'll stop, but at least I will know! I am paying attention to social cues. Low or poor self-monitors do not pick up on social cues.

Low self-monitoring is a key ingredient in making tough cookies. Tough cookies behave in ways that make sense for them, regardless of the situation. One reason for not adjusting their behaviours is because they don't see when they should or why. Low self-monitors are not ignoring the social cues; they don't see the social cues. This is one reason tough cookies are often surprised that others find them difficult to work with or to be around.

The Stress Response and the Fatal Flaw

I'm an extrovert. I talk. When I'm stressed, the volume increases. Some might say I yell. I have overused my trait of outward expression. Yelling is counterproductive. For me, extraversion has become a fatal flaw. Such is the case with tough cookies.

Often, people are promoted because they are good at their jobs. When promoted to manager, however, the rules have changed. Being a good employee does not ensure success as a manager. Managers must get results through others. You can't aggravate your employees and expect positive results.

Chapter 3: The Making of a Tough Cookie

I was a Tough Cookie

Prior to my work as an executive director, I was a counsellor. When I took on the leadership role of director, I was excited and nervous. What a new adventure! To top it off, I was going to work with the same colleagues I considered friends. It couldn't get better than that, or so I thought. Exit competent counsellor, enter fatally flawed leader.

As a counsellor, I was trained to watch for non-verbal cues and listen intently. It seemed I had a natural talent for reading people. I was confident. I was a self-starter. I relied on no one, worked hard, worried hard, took care of my own motivation, and liked things done yesterday. This worked well in the world of counselling. My strength was being strong with and for others. I had my people skills down pat. I was about to learn a very hard lesson.

As I started in my role as executive director, I set about learning the ropes. I had new responsibilities, new authority, and a new office. I was interviewed by the local paper and was asked, "What direction do you have for this Centre?" to which I replied,

"I will take my direction from the people for whom this Centre is built." Can you hear the harps and see the rainbows? Yep, I was optimistic, to say the least. I like harmony. Doesn't everyone?

As time went by, the position required new knowledge, skills, and abilities. The learning curve was steep. As challenges came my way, the stress increased. I increasingly accessed my interpersonal prowess. I thought by making people feel better, they would do better. I became more of a people-pleasing person than a leader. I was paying too much attention to how people were feeling and too little to what they were doing. I wanted staff to like me more than I was willing to give solid direction or hold difficult conversations about performance. This increased my stress further, which decreased my effectiveness even more. I started reading into things. I became a conspiracy theorist!

As executive director, I was responsible for all Centre operations. I found being accountable for what happened in all areas of the organization very stressful. I couldn't control what other people did in the same way that I had control over what I did in my previous position. I didn't know what they knew. I became increasingly aware that I didn't know much about the other positions. So, I started to ask questions—a lot of questions. I wanted to learn what each staff member did and how it was done. My Type A personality, however, turned inquiry into inquisition. My healthy attention to people-based detail became an unhealthy attention to other people's work, and I became a micromanager. People don't like micromanagers. I couldn't figure it out. Don't they understand that I need to know what's going on? It was coming across, however, as acting superior. I wasn't getting along, and I was hurt by the increasing isolation. So much for the harps and rainbows! What saved me were two things:

1. The strength of the staff
2. My not suffering from awarenessminusus and behaviourstuckedness.

I was not doing a good job, but I was a good learner. I recovered. I learned new skills and increased my trust in my staff. I let go and worked at being a better leader by reading books and taking courses on managing others. To make a long story short, we survived. I am forever grateful for the staff's patience and perseverance. Though it has been many years since leaving that position, I think of them warmly.

My experience is not unique. Many new managers stumble and even fail. When managers fail to recognize their impact on others and when that behaviour goes unchecked or unchanged, a tough cookie is born. I work with tough cookies because I was one. Many organizations, however, still do not recognize that management is a unique profession requiring training and education. Promoting people without leadership training because they were good at their jobs sets them up to fail. It's that simple.

How Do You Know if You're a Tough Cookie?

Consider the following:

a. What type of feedback have you been given? Have you discarded such feedback or discounted it in any way? Is there a pattern to the feedback you've received over time and by different people?
b. Be open to getting feedback by deciding how you can evaluate your performance as a manager.
c. Consider someone who you know does not like you or with whom you do not work very well. Invite her or him to lunch. Ask, "What are my fatal flaws?" They will be happy to tell you!

Look over the tough cookie types and ask yourself, "Am I a tough cookie?" Do I fit any of these descriptions, if I am brutally honest with myself? Remember, it's easy to identify tough cookie traits in others, but not so easy to see them in ourselves.

Chapter 4: The Cookies

Who are the tough cookies? How do they act? How do they communicate? How do others perceive them? Let's look at the types but with some qualifiers.

- No one fits any type exactly.
- Each cookie type is based on behavioural patterns, not the individual.
- A tough cookie in one situation may not be a tough cookie in another. "Gerald" found a job in a different environment and he fit right in. He was still a Ginger Snap but no longer a tough cookie!

1. The Ginger Snap

Out of all the tough cookies, Ginger Snaps are the most common. Why? They seem to be the ones that stand out and whose behaviours are the most contrary to respectful workplace guidelines.

Have you ever eaten ginger? Even when candied, ginger has heat. This tough cookie exhibits that trait. To those working with one, the Ginger Snap appears quick to anger. Whether the fuse is short or long, the Ginger "snaps," eventually. Ginger Snaps' behaviours foster fear and resentment. Employees fear reprisal.

The behaviour patterns that Ginger Snaps display include the following:

- Make overly direct comments
- Frequently express frustration and/or anger
- Use criticism as the method of providing feedback
- Tend to interrupt
- Express opinion as fact
- Like to take charge
- Take a "my way or the highway" approach to supervision
- Judge employees as "good" or "bad," rather than focusing on behaviour
- Have little patience with poor performance
- May intimidate others and appear to be a bully

I find that many people either love ginger snaps (the real cookie) or strongly dislike them. It is similar for this cookie type—you'll either get along with them or you won't. I believe it's because the person getting along with the Ginger Snap can take the heat and see beyond the snap.

2. The Black and White Cookie

There are many managers for whom grey does not exist. Their world is black or white, wrong or right, and rule-bound. Life is simple in the analytical, logical mind of the Black and White Cookie. You're paid to do a job, so do it. You're given standards, so meet them. No excuses. As for motivating employees? Why thank them for doing their jobs?

The behaviour patterns that Black and White Cookies display include the following:

- Set high standards and expect them to be met
- See the world from a logical perspective
- Have little patience with disorganization

- See many "reasons" as excuses
- Have a critical eye, see quickly what is wrong with a situation
- Employees feel criticized not coached
- Strictly enforce policies, standards, and duties
- Take a cookie-cutter (pun intended) approach to supervision by applying the rules exactly in the same way across circumstances and employees
- Find dealing with people draining because people are too complicated
- Create tension in conversations because others have a 50/50 chance of being wrong

Black and White tough cookies can be compassionate toward employees and allow for circumstance as long as it is right to do so.

3 The Hermit Cookie

Typically, we see a hermit as someone who has withdrawn from society. In the work world, employees see the Hermit Cookie manager as withdrawn. It is the absence of behaviour that is noticed. The behaviour patterns that Hermit Cookies display include the following:

- An absence of rapport, resulting in weak relationships with colleagues and employees
- Rarely ask for input when making decisions that impact others
- Would find the concept of walk-around management foreign
- May use avoidance as a conflict style, waiting for things to work out

- Tend to be introverted—retreats to the inner world of ideas and concepts
- Use email rather than direct communication
- Provide information on a "need to know" basis

4. The Oatmeal Raisin Cookie

Who doesn't like an oatmeal raisin cookie? It's a respectable cookie and one you can count on. No matter where you order an oatmeal raisin cookie, you get a cookie made of ... oatmeal and raisins. Oatmeal Raisin cookie managers exhibit the same traits. They are stable, someone we can count on, functional, and consistent. Too much of a good thing, however? The behaviour patterns that Oatmeal Raisin cookies display include the following:

- Resist change
- Use phrases such as those that follow:
  - "If it's not broke, don't fix it."
  - "We tried that years ago, and it didn't work then."
  - "Why reinvent the wheel?"
  - "We've always done it that way."
- Are single-minded to the point of resisting new ideas or processes and may even become the obstacle to change
- Instead of sweet surprises, raisins show up as occasional and surprising sharp jabs and critical remarks
- If they don't agree, they won't actively disagree; they just won't comply

5. The Fortune Cookie

What do you do with a Fortune Cookie? Whether you eat it or not, each one of us reads the message inside. As a little girl, I loved Fortune Cookies. It took me a while to figure out they weren't really telling fortunes. I figured Santa out before I figured out the cruel reality of the not-so-fortune-telling Fortune Cookie. So, what makes a Fortune Cookie one of the tough cookie types? It's in the messages. In the restaurant, the messages are pleasant. In the workplace, the messages are virtually always negative.

Although not written down on strips of paper, Fortune Cookie managers always have a message. The message comes through in what they say and do. The behaviour patterns that Fortune Cookies display include the following:

- Have a lot to say about problems, not solutions
- Use what has gone wrong in the past as evidence for predicting what will happen in the future
- Predict negative results before the results are in
- Often accused as being negative
- Counter others' optimism by being "realistic"
- Practice mind-reading by saying such things as:
  - "What you want is..."
  - "What he means is..."
  - "What she's really trying to do is..."
  - Make assumptions about others' intentions

6. The Imperial Cookie

The Imperial Cookie has jam in between two sweet, often melt-in-your-mouth biscuits. It's often associated with sitting and sharing a pot of tea and exudes a regal presence. Imperial Cookie managers exhibit behaviour patterns such as the following:

- Oblivious to how often they talk about
  their accomplishments
- They are never wrong and if you don't believe that,
  ask them
- Take credit for others' work

- Have a grandiose sense of self-importance
- If the facts don't support their statements, they say the facts are false
- If facts are indisputable, they will retract or modify their statements
- Say one thing but do another
- Speak highly of themselves but don't have the competencies to back up the boast

7. The Refrigerator Cookie

Not being a baker myself, I had heard of Refrigerator Cookies but really didn't know why they were called Refrigerator Cookies. Then I met a baker on a flight from Dallas to Calgary who said, "They have an ingredient that requires refrigeration. Let's just say they don't have a long shelf life." Refrigerator Cookie managers are equally as temperamental, and they exhibit behaviour patterns such as the following:

- Tend not to engage others and are more analytical than people-oriented
- "Spoil" when not refrigerated
- Little things become big deals
- Do not apply old skills to new environments very well

- Are normally calm and collected but will "melt" under pressure by becoming terse, critical, and impatient
- Need a controlled and organized environment
- Tend to lose organizational skills when stressed

8. The Shortbread Cookie

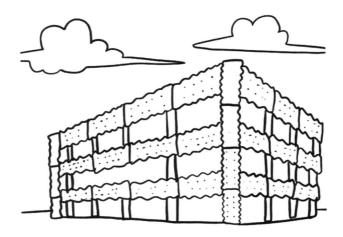

The Shortbread Cookie is one of the simplest cookies, involving only fat, flour, and sugar. Use inferior ingredients, however, and the quality of the cookie suffers. You can't make good shortbread with poor ingredients. You cannot have a successful company with poor leadership. Leadership is poor when it is short-sighted and focuses on short-term gain without considering the long-term ramifications. Shortbread Cookie managers exhibit traits such as the following:

- Out of touch with the "reality" of the employee's world
- Known for cutting budgets and resources while still expecting employees to perform and stay motivated
- Do not understand what it takes to motivate others
- Seem oblivious to the impact of change on those that work in the company
- Dictate changes
- Act as if the end justifies the means

- Do not consider the long-term impact of changes to the company
- Sacrifice long-term progress for short-term profit

9. The Double Chocolate Macadamia Nut Cookie (DCCMN)

At first, you might not recognize the DCCMN as being a tough cookie. You will, in all likelihood, be quite impressed. Most DCCMNs ooze confidence and charisma. They leave you with no doubt about how good they are. After a period of time, however, the sweetness becomes cloying and seems to overpower everything else. DCCMN managers may or may not be competent; it's hard to tell. They may or may not be sincere; it's hard to tell. Just don't take it for granted and don't turn your back. They have a way of needling or debasing you while appearing to support your efforts. Eventually, working with a DCCMN becomes confusing, frustrating, and overwhelming. In the end, you are either hooked on the sugar or develop distaste for chocolate chunks and macadamia nuts. DCCMN Cookie managers exhibit traits such as the following:

- Charisma and confidence devolve to vanity and arrogance
- Are self-absorbed, not self-aware
  - Tend to be out of touch with their impact on others
  - Place responsibility on others to give feedback—the onus is on the other person
  - Will disagree with the feedback or discount it
  - Will direct the conversations to their own accomplishments
- The "D" in the acronym might also stand for drama. There is plenty of drama in and around the DCCMN Cookies
- Do not walk the talk
- Have a pattern of people pulling back, pulling away, or breaking their interpersonal ties to them
- Would not agree to any of the above

10. The Chocolate Puff Cookie

The Chocolate Puff Cookie is a classic. It's not uncommon. You will find a version of the chocolate-crusted marshmallow—set on a firm wafer crumb base—in almost every store. Chocolate Puff Cookie managers are similar. Everyone knows someone who seems firm on the outside but soft on the inside. Chocolate Puff Cookie managers exhibit traits such as the following:

- Will reject, utterly, the concept of being soft-at-heart
- Equate soft-heartedness with being a pushover
- Speak firmly and directly to others

- Have been given feedback about being overly direct and abrasive
- Others are cautious and even uncomfortable around their "crusty exterior"
- Easily and forcefully express their opinions
- Are good at giving directions and assuming a leadership role
- Take a "no-nonsense" approach to situations
- Will entertain fewer friendships but are fiercely loyal to those who take the time to get to know them
- Are the first to help someone in need
- May not come across as soft-hearted, but their thoughtfulness is second to none

11. The Sugar Cookie

I asked a baker, "What happens when you burn sugar?"

She replied, "It changes colour and turns rock hard. If this happens, you can't salvage it. There is nothing you can add to turn it into anything you can use. Burn the sugar, and you have to start all over again!"

Sugar Cookie managers are much the same. They show up as caring and considerate, preferring a positive and harmonious work environment. If treated poorly, however, they become rigid and unyielding. Push them beyond their limits, and there is no going back! Sugar Cookie managers exhibit behaviours such as the following:

- Place emphasis on good relations with and among employees
- Accommodate others' needs easily
- Have excellent interpersonal skills
- Show they care about employees
- Work collaboratively with others
- Will become cold and distant if they feel their trust has been betrayed
- Will cut off all meaningful connections with the source of their pain
- May engage in uncommonly confrontational behaviour
- Appear numb to the plight of others who have "wronged" them
- Become increasingly critical and judgemental, using minimal responses, sarcasm, or caustic remarks when engaging with others in the broken relationship
- Will seek another job or position as a result of being "burnt"

12. Cookie Dough

How can Cookie Dough be tough? It's soft, gooey, and delicious. True, but Cookie Dough managers are also tough cookies. They are flexible but not firm. They would rather be friends than friendly. Cookie Dough managers exhibit behaviours such as the following:

- Have difficulty with disciplinary conversations
- Are concerned they won't be liked
- Accommodate by being flexible with guidelines, policies, and procedures
- Dislike absolutes and being put in a position where they need to place task accomplishment over individual need
- Avoid conflict at all costs

- Others may take advantage of them, reducing their effectiveness as a manager

Summary

Are you a tough cookie? Do you resemble any one cookie or are you a combination of cookies? Observe your behaviour and note the behaviours that define each type. Check off the ones that apply to you.

Observe those around you. Do you work with or for a tough cookie? Look only at behaviour and resist assuming the cookie's intention. No one knows the reasons any of us behave the way we do. Behaviour that makes sense to us will be perplexing to others. It is important to remember that we can change our behaviour, so improvement is always possible, if we are willing and able.

Chapter 5: So, I am Tough Cookie. Now What?

Congratulations! You're a tough cookie, and you know it. No easy feat! Did you discover this on your own? Did you decipher feedback that perhaps you had previously "overlooked?" Did someone, whose opinion matters to you break it to you gently? Did someone anonymously give you this book? Or, perhaps you're the person working with a tough cookie. Congratulations on reading this book. It will help.

Why Soft Skills?

Being able to apply soft skills requires emotional intelligence. Emotionally intelligent people are aware of and able to regulate their emotions, are self-motivating, and have greater empathy. Emotional intelligence differentiates between effective managers and poorly performing ones.[1]

---

1. Daniel Goleman, Emotional Intelligence (New York, New York: Bantam Dell, 1995).

Awareness of your emotions and the ability to channel them into positive actions is the foundation of emotional intelligence. This is bad news for some tough cookies. There are two problems with this:

a. The tougher the cookie, the harder it is to accept feedback and feedback is essential for behavioural change.
b. People hesitate to offer feedback to tough cookies—because of their very nature.

Even with feedback, it's still a long road to sustainable change. I have seen managers stumble and fall on their way to developing soft skills. The good news is, change is possible.

I worked with a manager who was unwilling and perhaps even unable to express positive emotions toward staff. Expressing positive emotions sounded like expressing feelings and feelings had no place at work! One day, he needed to attend a meeting. I went with him. As the discussions moved to a difficult topic, the manager was getting visibly angry. When asked what was going on with him, he said, and imagine him saying it slowly through clenched teeth, "They're called emotions."

It seemed more of a threat than a statement of self-awareness. Though the people around him were on edge with his response, I thought, *Wow, he actually admitted to having emotions. Now if he could just put that much energy into expressing friendly, rapport-building emotion.* It was a start.

Personality Change is Not Required

Although tough cookies must change their behaviours, per-sonality change is not required. Regardless of personality traits, behaviour is, by and large, under our control. For example, cheer-fully acknowledging a co-worker's "Good morning" is respectful behaviour even though you're not a morning person. Grunting, shrugging your shoulders, or not responding at all, is not. Seems simple enough, doesn't it? Seems to make sense, right? Common sense, however, is not common practice.

During a presentation, an audience member said, "You can't make me say good morning!"

To this, I simply replied, "If you work for me, I can." Needless to say, this person was a bit shocked. I continued, "It's really about understanding respectful behaviour." I went on to ask, "May I ask why you don't say good morning?"

The woman replied by citing the number of things that go wrong on her way to work. "The traffic is heavy, the roads are in bad shape, I have a long way to travel," and she continued with a few other reasons that obviously shaped her morning's experience.

"You don't understand," she told me, "It's never a good morning."

I took a chance with my next question. "What if I said hello instead? What would you do then?"

"Well, I'd say hello back," she replied as if I should have known the answer. Was this person a tough cookie? I don't know. However ... if I were a betting person ...

Our personality is not for others to judge. Our behaviour, however, is. I love the phrase, "What you think and feel is your business but what you say and do is the business of others."

We do not change our personality just because someone thinks we should. We don't wake up in the middle of the night with sudden enlightenment exclaiming, "Wow, I'm a difficult person!" Or, "Wow, I'm a tough cookie!" We modify our behaviour when we get feedback that something we are doing or saying is negatively impacting another. Or, at least, most of us do.

Tough cookies don't tend to change their behaviour unless there is a proverbial stick involved. Some significant event becomes the impetus for change. Perhaps Human Resources or the union becomes involved. Perhaps a friend's patience runs out. Perhaps the balance shifts to more behavioural "cons" than "pros."

Even if tough cookies' intentions are positive (and they often are), at some point, understanding tough cookies and being able to tolerate extreme behaviour runs our well of patience dry. Knowing that tough cookies mean well (and they often do) loses its impact in the light of incessant insensitive behaviour.

There are some tough cookies who will slightly modify their behaviour when the occasion fits, but it's not consistent. Being stuck in the philosophy of "That's just who I am" leaves little room to notice that "I am" is upsetting others. Strangely, these people seem proud of their perceived strength of personality. The lesson of the oak tree that breaks in a strong wind while the willow bends and remains unharmed seems lost on them.

Tough Cookies have Great Strengths

Given the descriptions and impact of tough cookies, you may be wondering, "Good grief, is there any hope?" Yes, there is, and it comes from the fact that tough cookies have great strengths and positive intentions that underlie their behaviours. The Ginger Snap, for example, wants to take action and get things done. The Black and White Cookie wants to get things done correctly. Regardless of the type of cookie, there will be a positive motivation behind the behaviours. The actions the tough cookies take to achieve their aims are not, however, positive.

So, what does this mean for tough cookies and your interactions with them? It means that tough cookies have great strengths and almost always have reasons that seem right to them for behaving as they do. For those of you working with tough cookies, it really helps to focus on their strengths. It modifies your judgement of who they are and helps you focus on what they do. And if what they do is having a negative impact, it is easier to address behaviour rather than personality.

Chapter 6: Strategies to Get You Started

First Steps for Tough Cookies

A tough cookie must raise self-awareness. Have you ever asked someone if they are angry and they rip your head off with the reply, "I'M NOT ANGRY!"? If so, you know what I mean when I talk about a lack of self-awareness.

You might protest and ask, "How can a person who is yelling not know they are angry?" True, the person knows his voice is raised but doesn't associate it with anger. It is a reaction, not a response. Reactive behaviour is common among tough cookies. Knowing what brings about the reaction is something they need to examine.

I ask my clients to work on the three areas of awareness using the phrase, "Notice, Notice, Notice." Like "location, location, location" being a well-used phrase about a key element in real estate, noticing is the key to building interpersonal skills.

Notice How You Communicate

This is a rough start for some tough cookies. First of all, they need to see the value of changing their behaviours. Secondly, they need to be able to modify their behaviours. A hefty degree of flexibility is required. Tough cookies need to be ready, willing, and able to adapt. If they can, they are on their way to developing soft skills. There are various ways to identify your own communication style:

1. Personality profiles (take several to get a well-rounded picture of your style)
2. Record a video of an interaction with others (with their permission)
3. Record an audio of your interactions with others (with their permission)
4. Ask a close friend for feedback
5. Reflect on feedback you have received in the past
6. Listen, really listen, to the sound of your own voice. Pay attention to your volume, speed, words you choose, the number of words you choose, and the tone of your voice.

Notice How Others Communicate

Noticing another's communication style is a form of empathy. Most people equate empathy with sympathy. Not true. Sympathy is feeling sorry for another; empathy understands the other's situation. This was good news for one tough cookie, who said, "This feeling thing, 1 don't like it!" What do you look for in another's style? There are a number of clues.

1. Notice how the person speaks. Does she speak softly and gently or loud and harshly?
2. What is her cadence? Does she speak rapidly or in a more measured fashion?
3. Does she use many words or get directly to the point?

4. What interests her? Can you tell by listening to the words she emphasizes?
5. What is her body language?

Being able to match another's style increases rapport and understanding. For example, if someone gets to the point quickly, matching that person's communication style means avoiding long, wordy explanations. Learning how to match is a skill all tough cookies need to master.

Notice Your Impact on Others

Has this ever happened to you? You are going to meet Mary for coffee. She walks in, relaxed, happy, and upbeat. As the conversation progresses, Mary starts to wilt. By the end of the "coffee," she slinks away, devoid of energy and enthusiasm. It's surprising how many of us don't notice our impact on others.

Not noticing your impact on others may not be a big deal for most, but for tough cookies, especially tough cookie managers, it is essential. Look for signs that indicate the other person is uncomfortable:

1. Looking away or down. Eye contact is culturally determined, so looking away or down may be a sign of respect or deference to authority.
2. Eyes wandering (e.g., looking at something else, looking at their phone, notebook, developing a sudden interest in the surrounding architecture)
3. You have said something, and it is followed by a sudden silence.
4. Yawning or sighing
5. Whispering to another person
6. Changing the subject
7. Not asking questions

8. Fidgeting

As a coach, I assign activities to raise self-awareness. The Mirror Exercise is one example.

The Mirror Exercise

Part A: Self-reflection
Looking in the mirror is not a metaphor. As a tough cookie, you really do need a mirror to use as a reminder to begin your self-examination. Purchase a pocket mirror. Keep it with you at all times. Look into it frequently. Put it on your desk. Open it so that you see yourself in it while you are working or interacting with others. What do you notice when you look in the mirror? What type of person is reflected in the mirror? What are you feeling?

I'll admit that many of my clients initially don't endorse the mirror exercise. Frequently, I hear this comment, "I know myself very well. Why do I need a mirror?" I explain that the mirror is not just an exercise in self-reflection; it is also a tool to measure openness and flexibility. Besides whenever someone exclaims that they know themselves so well that there is no new news, I worry.

Part B: Self-analysis
Having spent at least one week with the mirror exercise and noticing yourself, answer the following questions:

a. What are your strengths?
b. What are your challenges?
c. What areas do you think you need to develop? Why?
d. How do you think others perceive you?
e. What evidence do you have for your answer to (d)?
f. What feedback have you had from others about what you need to improve?

g. How would you describe your relationship with your colleagues? With those who report to you? With your supervisors? With your peers?

Take a week at the very least to answer these questions. Then reflect on your answers for a few days and return to your responses. Is there information that you would change, add, or delete? Do so.

Part C: Self-analysis

For at least another week, carry the mirror as before, but when you are in your office, turn the mirror away from you. This is a symbolic gesture for you to remember that this week you are focusing on two very important things:

a. Noticing the other person's state (seems happy, concerned, afraid, tenuous, cautious, frustrated, etc.)
b. Noticing your impact on him or her

Specifically consider and practice the following for one week:

a. Notice how you feel each day
b. Notice your reaction to others and/or situations
c. Notice how others are doing when you are in conversations with them. Are they melting? Are they in a better or worse state after having spent time with you? How do you know? What indicators do you use to answer these questions?

Start Small, People Get Suspicious

I instructed a course on management at a local university. Two people, obviously from the same organization, asked me if their manager had taken this course. I was curious, so I asked why they wanted to know. They said,

"Well our manager took a course and now she is much nicer. We are wondering if it was the course or if she just wanted something from us?"

People get suspicious! People have learned what to expect from tough cookies even if what they expect is the unexpected. For example, one might never be able to predict when a Ginger will snap but will prepare for the snap regardless. It's not so much the snap that does the damage but the never-ending anticipation. Relationships among people are like a dance. Change the dance and toes will be stepped on.

With one client, my initial suggestion was for her to smile when she interacted with others. In fact, I asked her to smile for at least 90 seconds in private before proceeding. "Practice, practice, practice" was to be her motto for the week. At our next meeting, I asked her how it went. She wasn't happy.

She said, "People looked at me strangely and even asked if I was feeling alright! Others just seemed uneasy. They seemed so shocked that I was smiling!" We discussed her previous pattern of interaction with others. She confessed she had never thought of noticing others' reactions to her communication style. She now recognized most people seemed distant or even fearful. It was an eye-opening experience. In this case, her employees gradually became less suspicious as she consistently continued to be more open and friendlier.

Recognize the Absence of Trust

Poor leadership handicaps a team. Employees will not follow leaders they don't trust, and tough cookies don't foster trusting relationships well. Either a trusting relationship is not of paramount importance or once having established it, maintaining is not.

At some point, a tough cookie will have to establish or re-establish trust. It's not an easy task, and there are many pitfalls along the way. Once trust has been broken, it's really difficult to mend and even then, the relationship is fragile. One mistake can send them back to square one.

Many of my clients struggle to adopt new relationship behaviours. They may not modify the behaviour enough to demonstrate a change or they may overshoot the modification, thereby seeming insincere. Although, seemingly counter-intuitive, when the manager attempts to do a better job at connecting, some employees may be more interested in getting revenge than supporting their leader.

I interviewed a large group of employees who were complaining to their organization. It was my job to identify the issues and make recommendations. The outcomes singled out a few common areas; however, the complainants were tremendously upset over one issue—leadership. I asked each employee the same question:

"If your organization was willing to do whatever it takes to establish a more positive work environment, what would you like to see more of or less of?" "Nothing, except firing the director! Anything else is too little, too late!" were the resounding responses. When interviewing the management team, common responses included the following:

"Why don't these people get a real job? Then they would see how good they have it here!"

I refrained from sharing the fact that over 80% of the employees saw little "good" about their work environment. In fact, the management team was described as intimidating, acting more like bullies than leaders. Clearly this was a toxic environment.

I presented my report. The message was not received well. The director and the management team did not believe the situation was that dire. The report was presented to the employees only after the team eliminated some sections and watered-down others.

Having no control once the report was given to the company, I was amazed as to the length the team would go to sanitize the report and blame the employees. A year or so later, I heard that the organization was forced to deal with the reality of its poor leadership and the resulting toxic work environment. It would be a long and expensive road ahead to regain any semblance of trust.

Overlearn New Skills

Overlearning new skills means you practice the behaviours at every opportunity. You become more at ease with them as you apply them in the right degree to the right situations. As one manager put it, "I didn't think much of this approach at first, but now it's second nature."

If you don't overlearn the new skills, you will default to previous behaviours when facing pressure, stress, and difficult situations. Then, yes, people will give up on you, shut down, and say "I told you it wouldn't last."

Another good strategy is to make an agreement with others whereby they will give you feedback should you revert to previous behaviour. Let them know that you welcome their feedback so that you can maintain positive behaviours and build trust. Developing and maintaining trust is essential. Openly communicating your intention to those around you is helpful.

First Steps if You are Working with a Practising Cookie

If the tough cookie in your life is working at changing behaviours, leave enough room for them to make mistakes. Coming down hard too soon may undo everything that has been done to this point. Perhaps you and the tough cookie can agree that you will supply corrective feedback. Would you agree to give feedback to the tough cookie? Do you know how to give effective feedback?

The Feedback Dilemma

Whether corrective or supportive, most people are reluctant to give the tough cookie any feedback. Most just avoid them entirely.

Corrective Feedback

There are three issues encountered when supplying corrective feedback:

1. It's a challenge to give feedback about specific behaviour without implying an assessment of the person.
2. We hint. Hints are often our trying to relay what's in our head without saying what's in our head. Tough cookies don't get hints.
3. Many times, we "correct" the entire group to avoid singling out one person. At a staff meeting, we may bring up the topic of respect in general terms, hoping that the tough cookie will get the message. This doesn't work. The tough cookie is the only one not realizing the message was for her.
4. We are hesitant to give feedback to a person of authority. If the tough cookie is the person in authority, many employees will see this as a "career-limiting decision."

The Going Forward Dilemma

A tough cookie modifies his behaviour. Others are relieved. Problem solved? No. Many times, the old relationship is maintained by the complainants themselves. Resentment and bottled up frustration results in carrying forward the initial relationship. It is understandable, but not productive.

I negotiated a communication agreement between a manager and her team. Going forward, the agreement allowed for a whistleblower to report should the manager revert to old behaviours. In addition, it allowed the manager to proceed on a clean slate with new employees by prohibiting discussion of the previous situation with new hires. When I checked in a few months later, I found that two employees had done exactly the opposite. They had found the time to relay, to new employees, the manager's prior negative behaviours.

One successful communication agreement between a manager and his executive assistant was a result of a willingness to comply. The manager was unaware how he was coming across to the employee. Through a mediated conversation, the manager asked the employee to indicate if and when if he was resorting to previous behaviours. They agreed on a statement that she would deliver that would serve as his cue to stop, reflect, and start again. It worked well because both were willing to move forward.

Chapter 7: The Ginger Snap

Summary of Strengths and Challenges

Strengths:

- Action-oriented
- Likes to get things done right the first time
- Communication is direct and to the point

Challenges:

- Impatient with others
- Can be overly direct; directness combined with anger may be seen as bullying others
- Rigid

Like a tornado, there is usually a path of destruction left by the snap of this tough cookie. In organizations, the path of destruction consists of grievances and complaints. The employees being supervised by the Ginger Snap might leave the company. Those that remain will be told, "That's just Darcy. That's just the way he is. You'll get used to it."

Employees don't dare give corrective feedback to the Ginger Snap. As the name implies, this tough cookie could snap at any point and an employee would not know when or why. Working with this uncertainty is stressful and demotivating. Improved performance, like the manager wants, has been squashed. The more the Ginger snaps, the lower the productivity. The lower the productivity, the more the Ginger snaps.

I know one Ginger Snap who is friendly and easygoing until poor performance sets him off. He becomes critical, sees reasons as excuses, and demands employees do more and do it better. A poorly performing employee will be up against an insurmountable force. Zero tolerance for poor behaviour plus maximum consequences make the formula for interpersonal interactions when a Ginger Snap snaps.

Another interesting phenomenon occurs in the wake of the Ginger Snap's interactions with others. An exclusive club is formed. Its membership consists of those who get along with the Ginger Snap. They are the fearless few who, for one reason or another, have earned the respect of the Ginger Snap. As a result, the Ginger Snap snaps less in their presence and interacts more openly, friendly, and without the underlying anger—at least, most of the time. What do these fearless few do differently than others? These are people who are not intimidated by the Ginger Snap's overly direct behaviour, or who at least do not show it. This is key to dealing with a Ginger Snap.

The Story of Bob

I worked with a Ginger Snap, Bob, whose situation was not uncommon. As a colleague, Bob was seen as a direct, straight-shooting communicator. With Bob, you knew where you stood. When Bob became a supervisor, however, his direct approach was not appreciated. Given authority, Bob became resented and feared by many of those reporting to him. He had turned on them, or so they thought. Frequent grievances required my interviewing Bob. He did not understand why he was resented for doing his job. As a manager, he had deadlines to meet, was accountable for performance, and was responsible for poor production.

Bob was using the qualities that got him promoted: efficiency, hard work, and high personal performance. He knew only one way. When the going gets tough, work harder and get tougher! He placed heavy demands on himself to succeed. He placed those demands on those reporting to him. Why did they complain when he pointed out their mistakes? Bob missed the fact that a manager is responsible for a lot more than performance. A leader is responsible to maintain morale, develop employees, promote teamwork, coach, maintain a respectful workplace, learn to do the right thing vs. doing things right and, oh yes, improve productivity. What Bob didn't know was that to improve productivity, he needed relationship skills. He needed to develop rapport, engage his direct reports, listen to their ideas, suggestions or complaints, and build trust. Bob didn't realize, as a manager, relationship behaviours are more important than technical competencies.

Strategies for the Ginger Snap.

If you recognize your type as a Ginger Snap and realize your management style is not working, you are halfway there. It takes a lot to admit responsibility for your behaviour. As leader, it is imperative that you are aware of your impact on others and be able to adjust your behaviour to different circumstances. Everything - and I mean everything - you do as a manager is magnified. What was acceptable before now becomes unacceptable because you are in the position of authority.

Remember the story of Bob? Colleagues appreciated his direct communication style. When he became a manager, however, his communication style seemed overly aggressive. He was now considered a bully. What changed? Expectations did. The team expected Bob to be "the same old guy", do his job instead of being responsible for theirs. As Bob faced the pressure of a new position, he became more task-oriented but this time their production was included. His behaviour became more extreme and those around him became less tolerant. Bob needed to adjust his behaviour. He needed to focus on building new relationships with those who had once been peers.

Ginger Snaps are my favourite tough cookie. They like being direct and they like others being direct with them. I can be honest and upfront with Ginger Snaps. I am able to share the following, directly:

1. It's not okay to show anger, frustration, or impatience, no matter what.
2. It is imperative to develop a relationship with each employee.
3. People will not tolerate dominating behaviour for very long.
4. Shift the focus from task-oriented behaviour to relationship behaviour.
5. The more you push, the lower the productivity.
6. Dominant behaviour creates resentment.
7. People will not learn well or perform well if they are afraid.

Strategies for Being Less Snappy

Ginger Snaps need to practice alternate behaviours:
1. Recognize reactions; start walking away.
   - Ginger Snaps need to walk away from the situation or distract themselves to avoid losing their cool. They need to recognize when they are starting to feel anger, frustration, or impatience. Catching the emotion arising is crucial. If you are a Ginger Snap, practice the following:

- Monitor your feelings. Know when you are starting to feel annoyed. This is a good time to take a break, cool down, and return to the situation later.
- Monitor your behaviour. Is your voice starting to rise? Are you talking faster? Are you interrupting? Do you hear yourself trying to push a point through? Are you saying "no" a lot and/or disagreeing? Are you talking more than you are listening?
- Monitor the other person's behaviour. Is the other person looking uncomfortable? Is that person becoming angry or shutting down?

2. Develop a relationship with your direct reports.
   - Develop rapport by getting to know each direct report.
     - Write down the name of each of your direct reports. List each person's strengths and areas to improve.
     - Determine what motivates each person and what demotivates him or her. Don't assume or guess. Meet with each direct report and ask him or her for this information. What barriers do they face at work? Are there any interpersonal issues that need to be addressed? Offer assistance.

3. People will not tolerate dominating behaviour for very long.
   - Let your team know you are working on being an effective manager.
     - Ask your team for feedback via a quick survey. Make it anonymous so each person can respond fully and honestly.
     - Give your team the results and let them know how you will proceed.

4. Shift the focus from task-oriented behaviour to relationship behaviour.
   - Complete the exercises from Chapter 6.

- Ask more questions of people versus telling them what to do.
- Practice giving out positive feedback to team members, both individually and as a team.

5. The more you push, the lower the productivity.
   - Use coaching skills to address performance.
   - Stop ordering and start asking people for their opinion. Listen to their responses. Agree on a course of action, together.
   - Know your personality style. There are many instruments that measure different aspects of your personality. Each one can help you identify when you are behaving in a non-productive way. Use this information to understand how others see you.

6. Dominant behaviour creates resentment.
   - Changing dominant behaviour to a more collaborative approach is pretty darned difficult. However, there are a few things you can do to help this along:
     - When giving feedback to others, remember this phrase: "Be tough on the problem, but not on the person."

7. People will not learn well or perform well if they are afraid.
   - You have to turn this around. There is no other way to improve performance.
     - Identify situations where you have modified your style. Do they exist? What allows you to be in control in one setting and not in another?
     - Understand others by observing how they prefer to communicate. Match their style to the best of your ability. For example, if a person gives a lot of detail, being direct and to the point could seem too aggressive. Soften your approach.

If You Are Working With a Ginger Snap

It is imperative that you do two things when dealing with the Ginger Snap:

1. Do not show you are intimidated.
2. Do not try to match the Ginger Snap's behaviour.

There is a fine line between not showing intimidation and excess push back. For example, let's say that a colleague suddenly looks at you and asks,

"What? Do you have a problem with this?"

You are frustrated, you have no idea what brought this on and frankly, you are a little tired of accommodating her direct approach. You react.

"You bet I do. Can't you just for once keep your opinion to yourself?"

Your reaction might be justifiable, but it won't help the situation. An assertive response will.

Assertive behaviour demonstrates respect for the other person's right to have an opinion as well as respecting your own right to disagree. Assertive responses show you are not intimidated without escalating the situation. Assertive behaviour in the above example would sound like:

"Are you interested in my opinion?"

An assertive response needs assertive body language. Your tone of voice should be direct but calm. Make direct eye contact. Square your shoulders. Stand or sit straight (Hint: If you are standing, turn your body slightly and only slightly away from the tough cookie. It helps you visualize the harshnes going past you). If the Ginger Snap snaps even more and says something like, "No bloody way!", then you are probably not dealing with a tough cookie, you are dealing with an angry person. A Ginger Snap by definition is someone whose behaviour may be overly direct, but whose behaviour is not intended to hurt, humiliate, or intimidate.

I facilitated a workshop in a very large room with a very large group. I was leading the participants through a formula for positive interpersonal interactions. A loud voice came from the middle of the room. I heard, "Genella, come here!" The volume of the request, I guessed, was not because of our geography. The participant was clearly frustrated.

I walked to the table (but inside I was cowering). I asked, "Yes, how can I help you?"

"What's this sh**?" he asked with only a slightly lower voice.

I responded with a direct tone of voice, "What stuff do you mean?"

I did not repeat his word. That would be negatively matching his behaviour. He pointed to the page in his workbook. "How did you get here?"

I turned to a recent page. I asked, "Did you complete this?" pointing to an exercise he clearly didn't finish.

"No" was the response.

"Okay, fill it in" I directed.

"Done", he said.

"Okay, now, if you take your answer to this and combine it with your answer to this (I pointed to the exercise), then you have the formula," I said simply and assertively.

"Ohhh, thanks", he said "I get it. Great!" and he thanked me again.

He spoke as if the proverbial, sh** had never happened. There was no big deal. He may have been a little frustrated, but I could tell he was never angry.

The difference between a Ginger Snap and an angry person lies in the tough cookie's consistent behaviour. Yes, a Ginger Snap can become angry like anyone else, but mostly he or she is just being direct. The directness becomes problematic when it is misapplied through a lack of self-awareness and a lack of flexibility.

Chapter 8: The Black and White Cookie

Summary of Strengths and Challenges

Strengths:

- Logical
- Discerning—can clarify a confusing situation by applying rules and regulations
- Good decision maker
- Task-oriented with high standards

Challenges:

- Has difficulty with situations that require going beyond rules and regulations
- If it isn't clearly defined, a concept is difficult to understand
- Can be overly analytical
- Can seem cold, unfeeling, and quick to criticize

I was happy to learn that there was a cookie officially called the Black and White Cookie. In fact, the Black and White Cookie is a New York, NY, favourite. Although the actual cookie may not be well-known, the tough cookie human is. How many people do you know who see the world as black and white? If it's not right, it must be wrong. Grey areas present them with a dilemma and dilemmas are daunting. They solve the dilemma by applying rules, regulations, and policies. Just because Black and White Cookies are strongly analytical, it does not follow that they are accurately analytical. Doing things right is a black and white approach. Doing the right thing is something different. The right thing requires a person to weigh all aspects of a situation. It goes beyond the rules, recognizes special circumstances and challenges the status quo.

Black and White Cookies, like all tough cookies, are misunderstood. They are often seen as unfeeling and critical. They are not unfeeling and being critical, in their world, is a good thing. How else would you meet standards? How else would you know what is going wrong so it can be fixed? The world needs people who can be objective and discerning but by relying too much on logic to make a decision, the tough cookie will fail to recognize its impact on people. By focusing solely on what is wrong with a situation, the tough cookie comes across as hypercritical. The manager creates employees who become resentful and fatigued with this approach. Ken Blanchard calls this a seagull manager[2]—one who swoops in, dumps on you, and leaves. Blanchard encourages managers to "catch people doing something right" and redirect undesirable behaviour. Catching people doing something right? A Black and White Cookie might see that as a waste of time. I know one Black and White Cookie who did.

---

2. Ken Blanchard, Whale Done! The Video, (Clive, IA: Ken Blanchard / Sollah Interactive, 2002).

The World According to Alex

Alex was good at her job. In fact, she was so good that when a promotion to management came up, she was the obvious choice. Alex had a critical eye. She could analyze a situation and come up with a creative solution. She was cool under pressure and diligent in her work. She called herself a perfectionist, using the description in such a way as to relay her high standards and expectations. The high standards she set for herself served her well. She was considered a top performer. She needed and wanted little direction. She was independent, consistent in her work, and dedicated to reaching the company's goals. As a manager, however, her strengths became her fatal flaws.

Alex was promoted to a unit manager. She was responsible for the unit's meeting production standards in a time when they had to do more with less. Resources were tight and demands were high. Vacated positions weren't being filled immediately, if at all. It was stressful. Employees were stretched to the max and it started to show. Morale dropped. Employees were burnt out. As one employee said, "I could keep going if I knew there was a light at the end of this tunnel." Another employee questioned whether or not they were achieving any of the company's goals. Most wanted to know if the pressure from scarce resources was going to continue forever. To say the team felt "out of the loop" was an understatement.

Alex's solution was for everyone to work harder, work smarter, and just keep going. In order to meet their goals, she needed to improve efficiency. In order to improve efficiency, she had to find out how employees could improve their performances. In order to do this, she had to find out what they were doing that was inefficient, point it out, and change it. This didn't work too well, for reasons that seemed obvious to everyone except Alex.

Production in the unit was decreasing and employees were repeatedly upset whenever Alex corrected their behaviours. The constant corrections came across as overly critical and, since they weren't balanced with positive feedback, people rebelled. Grievances were filed, and the union demanded the company do something about Alex. Enter executive coaching.

I met with Alex who grudgingly agreed to be coached. As with the Ginger Snap tough cookie, I had the opportunity to be direct, but I had to do it logically! I needed to leave out an impassioned plea of asking Alex to be less of a task manager.

As we worked together, Alex's genuine feelings for the employees began to surface. She cared. I asked her why this concern was not apparent. She explained that time was too valuable to be wasted on commending people for doing their jobs. She needed to focus on improvements.

"Besides," she said, "showing my concern involves feelings, and I don't do feelings very well. They don't get the job done, hard work does." Alex listened when I reported research showing that happy employees are more productive. Having happy employees increases the company's profit. She understood, but that didn't make it any easier for her to give positive feedback. My homework for Alex was difficult for her to complete. It was not connected to logic, as she defined it, and it dealt with feelings. Below are strategies that Black and White Cookies can use to balance their task and relationship behaviours.

Strategies for Black and White Cookies

Like the Ginger Snap, it is important for Black and White Cookies to enter the world of rapport.

1. List your direct reports. List what you believe motivates and demotivates each team member.

2. Let your team know that you will be finding out a little bit more about their experiences in their job including any obstacles to completing their tasks. Let them know you would like them to be completely honest as you value their input. Emphasize that you will be asking about your performance. Let them know that you realize you could be doing a better job and want to make the changes each team member needs.

   i. Hand out a brief questionnaire with the following questions:

      1. On a scale of 1–10 (with 1 being completely dissatisfied and 10 being completely satisfied) how satisfied are you with your job?

      2. What would make it a _____? (add one number to their response)?

      3. On the same scale of satisfaction, how satisfied are you with me as your supervisor?

      4. What would make it a _____? (add 0.5 to their number)

   ii. It is important, very important, that you do NOT focus on what numbers are given. What IS important is the second part to the requested score. That is, what would make it a _____? In the first part, you will be gathering information about their job, thereby knowing what to improve. The second part contains data for you as a tough cookie. But what if they are not telling you the truth?

   The employee, especially if he or she is dissatisfied, may not tell you the truth. After all a) you are the supervisor and b) you haven't done a good job in building trust! It is an apparent flaw because I designed it that way. If the employee feels you are doing a good job, they will give you ... let's say an 8. If the employee is afraid, resentful, or dissatisfied, he or she may still give you an 8 or higher. Doing so would keep them safe and avoid having to discuss this with you in detail.

Asking the question, "What would make it an 8.5?" is a golden question. Listen, really listen to the answers; this is your evidence. Listen to how the employee will shrug it off, be hesitant to speak, give you some information about some trivial matter, or dive in and tell you what he or she really thinks. Regardless, encourage at least one answer, don't minimize even a trivial response, and thank the person who tells you their truth. Then ensure you meet that expectation. Ensure you raise the rating by 0.5 by doing what they ask of you. Let them know that you will follow up with each of them in a month to see how you are doing.

In Alex's situation, she was concerned about how much time she was spending in this exercise when deadlines loomed. I replied that the deadlines wouldn't be met as the team continued to lack leadership. Building rapport and encouraging the team members would only help the situation. Simply put, it wasn't working her way.

3. When meeting with each team member to discuss their answers to the questionnaire, ensure you ask them what motivates them at work and what demotivates them. Check your list. Were you right for all employees? What did you learn from this exercise?

4. Catch people doing something right. That's it, full stop! I asked Alex to find three positive things about someone each day and let them know. This was very difficult for her at the beginning. You need to continue this ... forever. If it doesn't become second nature to you, you aren't trying hard enough!

5. Review research by reading books on leadership. Each will show how leadership impacts employee performance and how good leadership needs rapport, trust, and relationship building.

6. Reflect on a time when recognition was meaningful for you. Who recognized you? For what? How did it feel? If it was meaningful, it would have felt good. Extend this courtesy to your team members. Employees who feel good do not slack off, they work harder.

7. Find out more about your personality style. It is good to realize how you see the world. It is one perspective and not necessarily the perspective.

8. Consider a break for a team-building. Use personality styles and have everyone identify and share their type.

9. Above all, show you care about your team members as persons and not just about what they produce.

If You Are Working With a Black and White Cookie

Do not take their critical feedback personally. This is much easier said than done. Some strategies that may help include the following:

1. Do not show you are intimidated.

2. Remind yourself that the Black and White Cookie is trying to help by pointing out what you are doing wrong. It is based on the tough cookie's intent, it's not personal.. The Black and White Cookie, as opposed to getting things done, wants to get things done right.

3. Thank them for the feedback even though it sounds like criticism. Ask the Black and White Cookie for some positive feedback. Simply ask this cookie, "What am I doing right?"

4. Request permission to provide feedback. For example, "Thanks for letting me know what to improve. May I make

a request?" ["Sure" is the likely response]. "Good, thanks. When you point out what I am doing wrong in front of others, I get frustrated. I would appreciate it if you talked to me one-on-one about how to improve. In that way, I can ask you questions, or you can show me what I'm supposed to change." This request is framed in the classic, "When you ... I feel ..." statement. These are called "I" messages. Many people report that a) it sounds too scripted, and b) you don't make requests like that of your supervisor.

If it feels scripted, you have to make it your own. That is, using your style and specific words that reflect your style and the situation at hand.

It is true that some leaders dislike any improvement feedback, but Black and White Cookies are not mean-spirited. They are logical. If you show them how to make things better, they will usually comply. If you get a very negative response, remember, you are not working with a tough cookie, you are working with a mean-spirited person who should not be in a management position. Tough cookies can be mean-spirited, but most tough cookies are people over-using their strengths and not flexing their behaviour to meet the situation.

Both the Ginger Snap and the Black and White Cookie direct their energies outward. There are cookies, however, who do just the opposite. When the going gets tough, the tough go inward. The Hermit Cookie is a great example.

Chapter 9: The Hermit Cookie

Summary of Strengths and Challenges

Strengths:

- Radiates calmness in the middle of a crisis
- Allows people to determine how to complete their tasks
- Willingly delegates duties for employee development

Challenges:

- Tends not to share information
- Is out of touch with team morale and concerns
- Withdraws and shuts down when challenged
- Will feel pressured by the need to demonstrate personal connections with employees

You would think that the Ginger Snap or the Black and White Cookie would present the toughest challenge. Strangely enough, it is the Hermit that causes the deepest resentment among employees. In the case of the Hermit Cookie, what he or she doesn't say and doesn't do is the source of much frustration.

"Hermits originally were a plain cookie with spices and raisins, or currants added."[3] When I looked up the Hermit Cookie, I found there were countless varieties. Some used dates, some didn't. Others used brown sugar instead of white. Commercial hermits are rolled out and cut into bars. So many varieties, yet what connected them was a) people like them and b) they are easy to make. I have found this to be true for most of the Hermit cookies. When dealing with Hermit Cookies one-on-one, they are generally quite pleasant and by "easy" I mean they like things low-key and tend not to get upset quickly.

"Hello? Where are you, Patrick?"

I was hired to help Patrick develop stronger interpersonal skills. Patrick was a Hermit Cookie. My first communication from Patrick was via email. I had requested a meeting and his reply was brief and to the point requesting a coffee shop location. He didn't want others to see he was being coached. We set a meeting date.

As luck would have it, however, on the day I was to meet Patrick, the roads were icy, and there was a strong north wind blowing snow over the highway. When you live on the prairies, you get used to this. So, this was just another day on my way to work. The roads got worse. I had to slow down, and I was going to be late. I pulled over to call Patrick. He was already at the coffee shop. I informed him about the situation and that I was going to be about a half hour late. I asked him if he still wished to keep the appointment. Silence (except for the wind).

"Well, I've booked out the time and can extend it, so yes we can still meet" he said.

"Okay," I said. "I will keep going. See you in about 30 minutes." Silence.

---

3. Mary E. Gage, "Hermits," New England Recipes, accessed October 24, 2018, http://newenglandrecipes.org/html/hermit-cookie.html

"That's fine," came the eventual reply but I detected something in his voice that seemed to indicate it was not fine.

"Are you sure?" I pressed. "We can reschedule."

Silence.

The reply was curt. "No, I don't want to reschedule."

The conversation ended abruptly.

Sure, I thought. "Don't ask how I'm doing. Don't ask if I should keep going. Don't be concerned about the weather. Don't be concerned about anything other than your schedule! Perhaps the cold weather was freezing my ability to be objective and shortening my patience ... slightly.

I pulled up to the coffee shop about 25 minutes later. I walked through the door and spotted a man with a notepad looking directly at me. I walked towards him. He got up and shook my hand. "How are you?" he asked. "I was a bit worried about your driving in this weather."

Duh. Okay, Genella, pick your jaw up off the ground, I instructed myself. "Fine and thanks," was my reply.

We sat down, and he said, "I ordered you a hot tea or would you like a coffee?"

Clunk was the sound of my jaw hitting the ground a second time!

"Tea would be fine. Thanks!" I managed to reply. With tea, a warm environment, and a very friendly client, I thawed—literally and figuratively. We spoke for a bit about coaching and the circumstances surrounding his company's request. He admitted that he had been reluctant at first to meet with me but realized it was probably a good idea. We set goals and a schedule to meet.

Before we left, I stated, "You know, you are not nearly as rude as you come across. In fact, you are quite pleasant." He didn't seem surprised.

Rather, he asked, "What gave you that impression?"

"Which part?" I teased him slightly.

"Both," he replied.

I described the brief and to-the-point emails we had exchanged. I noted how they were devoid of any salutation or ending with his name attached to closing such as "Sincerely" or "Regards." I described my perception of our phone call. I also described his actions when we met and his caring approach.

"I guess that is why we are meeting," he admitted, "I'm not good with people and tend to avoid emotional expressions. I'm told I am too stand-offish." It was a good meeting and a great start to our coaching. Even the weather improved.

Part of my work with Patrick involved meeting with each of his direct reports. There were a dozen managers that looked to him for leadership. Each one relayed much the same story. Patrick spent more time in his office than he did talking to and checking in with the managers. Some managers openly resented him and said he was too laid-back and perhaps even lazy. Others admitted he was a nice guy but completely out of touch with what was going on. The common concerns were as follows:

- Spends too much time in the office
- Doesn't "have our back"
- Gives little guidance and less appreciation
- Does not share information
- Doesn't react or respond to requests from managers
- Finds excuses for the way things are between him and the management team
- Utterly uninvolved

The depth of these concerns was surprising to Patrick. He stated that managers should be allowed to do their jobs the way they saw fit. They were the experts in their areas and he had his own work to do! Understanding how leadership differed micromanagement was difficult for Patrick. He felt that any input from him would be considered out of line or micromanaging. He needed to learn how to support his managers and lead the team. He needed to go against his natural tendency to retreat when he was needed most.

The Not-so-Open-Door Della

Della worked in a very small office with a single administrative assistant. She had an office and the assistant had a desk just outside her door. Two people, one small space, and the beginning of a conflict.

The support person complained. It seemed that almost all contact between the manager and herself was done through email. She said she felt frustrated because there were times when she would have liked to have had a face to face meeting, but this was not encouraged.

Della didn't understand the complaint. "I have an open-door policy," she stated. "I just find email more efficient."

I asked her, "What about the sign on the door?"

"What of it?" The manager seemed miffed.

"It says," I pointed out, "Please knock and wait to be acknowledged before entering. Do you think that might have something to do with being seen as unapproachable?"

Hermits like their caves. They do their best work when they are alone. Getting to know this manager as I did, I was surprised she let anyone in the office at all.

Strategies for Hermit Cookies

As with Patrick and Della, Hermit Cookies need to fight their natural tendency to withdraw when under pressure. They withdraw not just physically, but also mentally and emotionally. Others interpret this as a lack of concern or interest and a lack of leadership. Metaphorically, the ship is afloat without a captain at the helm. Chaos and concern reign. A ship needs a captain to keep it afloat in turbulent waters and to interact with the crew. How can a Hermit Cookie learn to be a strong captain? This type needs to consider the following strategies:

1. Understanding personality type
   a. An introverted person is less expressive than an extrovert. Hermit Cookies will more than likely score as an introvert. Knowledge of personality allows the Hermit to shed the pressure of needing to be someone else. Rather, they understand what is required is a change in behaviour and not a change in personality.
2. Set up a routine to interact with the team.
   a. The more pressure you feel about having interact, the less likely you will do it. A routine is essential.
      i. Write down different ways to interact with the team and execute those strategies. Mix up the type of interaction but make interaction a routine. Examples of interacting with others are as follows:
         - Say good morning.
         - Walk around and check in with team members to see how each one is doing.
         - Ask open-ended questions when interacting with others to maximize dialogue.
         - Relay information that impacts each department or team.
         - Hold weekly meetings; encourage attendees to bring forward any concerns that may benefit from a group brainstorming session.
         - Walk around; stop and talk about what's happening. Listen (really listen) to their answers.
3. Learn to ask more questions; use a coaching style of leadership.

4. Find one thing you have in common with each team member. Speak to that commonality...occasionally.

5. Meet with each team member. Find out the following:

   a. What is meaningful about his or her job?

   b. What is frustrating about his or her job?

   c. How can you help?

   d. Share your thoughts on his or her performance (only good stuff) and note how he or she reacts.

   e. Call a spade a spade. Let your team know that you realize you're a hands-off leader but want to be there for them. Agree upon a phrase that clearly indicates the team member needs assistance on a task or in a situation. For example, a team member may agree to say to you, "Pat, I really need help on this one," which would be your cue to get out of your shell.

6. Show appreciation for each team member's effort. Use the following guidelines:

   a. Make recognition personal. Avoid the cookie-cutter (pun intended, yet again). My dog's is named Tucker, and I don't eat processed food. Giving me a treat for Tucker would mean a lot. Giving me a gift certificate to a local, fast-food restaurant would not be meaningful. (Except if they served ice cream. I consider ice cream a health food ... sort of ... oh, who cares ...)

   b. Make recognition about specific behaviours. Notice what people do and acknowledge when they have "gone the extra mile". Notice when one team member supports another. Show your appreciation.

   c. Make recognition timely. Recognize effort and good work as close to the event as possible. Watch for opportunities to let the team members know that what they do matters.

d. Use recognition often. Those not gifted in the art of appreciating others will say that recognition becomes meaningless if employees are thanked too often. Authors, Kouzes and Posner, state that in their many years of research, no one has ever complained about being thanked too much![4]

e. Understand that a failure of recognition contributes to low morale and poor performance in the organization. Also understand that you make a difference when you, as leader, express your appreciation.

If You Are Working With or Know a Hermit Cookie

The most effective strategy you can take with a Hermit Cookie is not forcing interaction. The more pressure a Hermit feels, the more he or she will retreat. So, the more you want to talk about a matter, the more the Hermit will want to stay silent. This is especially true in issues of conflict. While it's understandable, don't assume the Hermit doesn't care. Aloof behaviour is not indicative of a lack of concern. It is, rather, indicative of the lack of an ability to show it.

Ask for what you need. Make a direct request. Be simple, clear, and non-threatening. You may be surprised to get a response that is inconsistent with your assumptions. If requests are clear, direct, and to the point, the Hermit Cookie will respond.

---

4. James M. Kouzes & Barry Z. Posner, The Leadership Challenge: How to Make Extraordinary Things Happen in Organizations, 5th ed. (San Francisco: Jossey-Bass, 2012).

Chapter 10: The Oatmeal Raisin Cookie

Summary of Strengths and Challenges

Strengths:
- Is often the employee that holds the "corporate memory"
- Works hard
- Has great experience and insight
- Will stick with status quo, so changes are not made in rush or error

Challenges:
- May refuse to see the need for change
- Becomes very stubborn if he or she doesn't agree with the change
- Does not react well to pressure or being rushed to new ideas or new processes
- Will put up obstacles to prevent him or her from having to make changes
- Can be very critical of others or of processes if pressured to change

Oatmeal Raisin cookies have subtle traits that land them in the tough cookie category. You won't get a reaction from them if you are looking for expressed frustration or even an argument. Leave that to the Ginger Snaps. Oatmeal Raisin Cookies like things stable and resist change. If you have ever tried to remove oatmeal that's been left too long in the pot, you will realize how sticky and resistant it can be. Add pockets of sweetness and presto, an oatmeal raisin cookie.

These cookies are comforting and familiar. It's a cookie that you can count on for taste. It's like the vanilla flavour of the ice cream world. They are soft, but not too soft, chewy but not too chewy, and sweet but not too sweet. You might even say it's a nice cookie. How can such a nice cookie, therefore, be used to describe some not so nice behaviours? As with the other tough cookies, too much of a good thing is no longer a good thing.

Oatmeal Raisin tough cookies can become too stable. When they become set in their ways, they become virtually impossible to change. They often refuse to see alternate ways of doing things. Like the dried oatmeal that sticks to the pot with the consistency of cement, this tough cookie gets stuck on what not to change. Just try getting cement to flex!

Remember the pockets of sweetness? Under pressure, the sweetness is replaced by subtle yet caustic remarks under the guise of humour. To others it is plainly, harsh sarcasm.

A friend of mine began using email about seven years ago. Do the math. Email has been out for a little longer than that. What caused this tough cookie from refusing change to saying, "I will email you"? The system. His email account kept crashing because it was loaded down with hundreds of emails. Slowly he progressed from emailing, to attachments, and I have heard he is now scanning!

The Story of Dug-in Don

Don was the person in the organization that everybody knew and respected for his experience and knowledge. He had worked for the company for more than 25 years. He was pleasant when interacting with others, supportive of other colleagues, and by and large made a good supervisor. When people met Don, they liked him. Working with Don when there was a shift in policy or procedure, however, was another story. When the going got tough, Don became a tough cookie!

I worked with Don indirectly. I was hired by a company to develop a training and coaching program that would help a team of supervisors lead change. Don was part of that group. The company was going through a major restructuring that would impact everyone, from front-line workers to senior leaders. A new CEO was hired to implement the restructuring. I met with each supervisor to collect the information I needed for customizing the program. The leadership program, as a result, focused on developing supportive relationship skills and managing change. When I met with Don, I understood why the other supervisors identified him as one of the challenges.

Don was not so much of a tough cookie toward the people he supervised. He became, however, a very tough cookie to those who supervised him. His peers were surprised at Don's reaction to the new processes. Don, up to this point, had not shown up as a stubborn person. Now, following the change, Don's reactions ranged from distant discontent to outright refusal to adopt new procedures. In addition, although his comments when discussing about the new processes were few, they targeted any possible flaws. Don was very intelligent and had plenty of experience. He could find flaws. To some degree, Don's supervisors worked around his reactions, honouring his expertise and many years of service. There were limits, however, and when they were reached, Don had the choice to adapt or face disciplinary action. Don adopted the new procedures, slowly. Eventually, he settled back into being the more familiar, amiable colleague and employee. His sharp wit and resulting sharp comments, however, surfaced every now and then.

To the new CEO, Don may have appeared as a problem employee! Don would not have agreed with that assessment. He described himself as efficient for evaluating new procedures. To others, his "If it ain't broke, don't fix it" approach was seen as his opposing change in any form. He didn't. He needed time to evaluate what was being asked of him by questioning the process and comparing it to how things currently worked. Oatmeal Raisin Cookies are like that. They hold onto what they believe is of value, what has worked in the past, and live by the values they have come to realize. New ways don't need to replace the old way of doing things just because they are new.

Strategies for Oatmeal Raisin Cookies

Oatmeal Raisins who have not had their extreme behaviours pointed out will not be interested in this book. Ever. You are reading this, so here are five strategies to get you started.

1. Consider that not all changes are bad; some might be quite well thought out!
2. Take time to understand that others around you may not see what you see or know what you know. Consider using your knowledge to improve upon the changes that are taking place.
3. Look for something good in the changes. Where are the opportunities to develop a new skill, help more people, or be more efficient, etc.? Start small. Look for just one thing.
4. Learn why things are changing and what the new procedures are to accomplish.

5. Consider listening as much to others as you would have them listen to you.

6. Refrain from sarcastic remarks as a way to prove your point.

Of all the cookies described in this book, it is the Oatmeal Raisin that surprises people. There is a big difference between an Oatmeal Raisin cookie and an Oatmeal Raisin tough cookie. What was once stable becomes inflexible. What was once easygoing becomes combative through low-key but ongoing resistance to change. Finally, what was once an accepting person becomes someone who can move forward only when they understand and endorse the change or are mandated to do so. Who knew?

If You Are Working With or Know an Oatmeal Raisin Cookie

The following strategies are ways to "unstick" the Oatmeal Raisin's resistance.

1. Don't push. You will get stuck in the cement as it slowly hardens around you.

2. Don't expect the Oatmeal Raisin to accept new procedures or structures without knowing the reason why.

3. Do ask the Oatmeal Raisin what he or she thinks. Use the knowledge and experience to improve procedures. Give him or her the opportunity to point out what might be flawed.

4. Do encourage the Oatmeal Raisin to advise rather than criticize.

5. Be prepared to have the Oatmeal Raisin speak directly, perhaps even critically.

6. Don't show you are intimidated by the resistant behaviour. Rather, show you value his or her input.

7. Give the Oatmeal Raisin time to evaluate the changes. Expect faultfinding.

8. Listen to the Oatmeal Raisin's concerns. Acknowledge them.

9. Sell the problem before you try to sell the solution. The Oatmeal Raisin will be more receptive if you show how a change in things such as technology, resources, generational differences, or even societal norms has created new challenges that need new solutions.
10. Do give the Oatmeal Raisin the opportunity to explain or defend his or her position when opposing change. There may be a valid reason for the apparent resistance.
11. Remember that Oatmeal Raisins have a purpose. They are good in the trenches and they get things done. Don't let their value be lost.
12. Do have clear boundaries and expectations of agreement.

Chapter 11: The Fortune Cookie

Summary of Strengths and Challenges

Strengths:

- Often low-key
- Steady
- Solid individuals
- Have Plan B in their pockets because Plan A probably won't work.

Challenges:

- Each Fortune Cookie is slightly different.
- One may be very critical and resistant to any change (because it won't work anyway) while others may be less outwardly critical but still harbour negativity within.
- They will first see what is wrong with a situation, and predict negative results before the results are in.
- As a leader, this cookie tends to create low morale. Fortune Cookies, whether in the position of leadership or not, have a big impact on the work environment.

The Fortune Cookie is one that others see as "the negative person." As a result, it is difficult to identify their individual strengths since they are masked by the "glass is half empty" view of the world. In fact, almost anyone can become a Fortune Cookie – just be a "doomsayer." The Fortune Cookie will use past catastrophes as evidence to predict future outcomes!

This tough cookie's attitude is draining but they tend to mask it with a degree of levity. A message surrounded by something sweet. Common phrases include:

- I was just joking
- You're too sensitive
- You've got to get a thicker skin if you're going to work here
- "He thinks..." or "she feels..." or "they want..."

These last phrases indicate where the Fortune Cookie shifts into being a fortune-telling cookie. This tough cookie seems to know (or thinks they know) what another is thinking, feeling, or wanting.

In my workshops, I often ask if anyone has ever worked with a negative person? Judging by the numbers of hands that shoot up, there are a lot of negative people out there. And, this cookie impacts others. Fortune Cookies have strong opinions on what is going to happen (and it's never good), who is going to get fired (because they heard it somewhere), when the company is going under or expanding too quickly, etc., etc., etc. You get the message.

Fortune Cookie Scenario

You and all your team members are going out for lunch to celebrate reaching a milestone in a project. There are ten people on this team, including you. The group has decided to go for Chinese food. It is a good meal, good conversation and an all-round good celebration. Relief! Before the meal is ended, a dish of Fortune

Cookies is passed around. Each person takes a cookie and breaks it open to read the message inside. Each person reads their message out loud.

The first person reads, "You are lucky to have met your project deadlines. No really, it was luck!"

Everyone laughs. The second person reads their message. "The first part of the project was easy. Now the work begins."

Everyone laughs, but not quite as heartily. Now, the third person reads, "It's frustrating when not everyone works equally hard on your team. Look around…"

Laughter is hesitant. You start asking questions. "Is this a joke?" or "Okay, who rigged the Fortune Cookies?"

The fourth message is read. "It would be nice to be rewarded but the company does not want to set a precedent. So, nice work but no reward."

No laughter. Uneasiness builds. The fifth cookie is broken open and contains the following message: "If you do your job too well, you will be stuck having to work that hard forever!"

Doubt begins to plague the group.

"No, seriously, is this a joke?" someone asks outright.

"Let's see what the next one says," another person demands. "Maybe it turns around!"

"It's not going to turn around," reads the sixth cookie. "This is as good as it gets."

"Wha-a-a-t?" someone shouts. "How do these darn cookies know what we do at work or what we are saying, now?"

Another team member shakes their head. "This has to be a coincidence!"

One more cookie is broken, and the piece of white paper is pulled out. "Coincidences are for fools," it reads.

"That's it!" exclaims the holder of the eighth cookie. "I want to know right now. Who set up this joke? It's not funny. This is supposed to be a celebration! How about telling us now?" No one steps forward. The eighth cookie is opened.

"The new people will experience great resistance to their ideas", it read.

"This is not only weird but it's kind of a downer," admits one of the new team members. "I still have a cookie. Here goes," he says as he breaks open the second last cookie and reads the message, "But don't worry, those who have been here longest will train the enthusiasm right out of them."

"Someone has a twisted sense of humour" the team member with the final cookie protests. "Okay, this is the last one. Let's hope we find out who set this up," he says hopefully. He reads it aloud. "I am a Fortune Cookie, and I can turn a situation from fair to foul in the blink of an eye."

The team leaves the celebration with celebration now only a distant memory. The poor team! It's okay. This is a fictional story. It's not that bad in real life, or is it?

"I'm Forced to Be Here" Sandy

The following example of a Fortune Cookie's impact is not specific to a workplace but rather to a workshop. In my workshops, I ask participants to share what they would like to get out of the course. Most responses, logically, are connected to the workshop topic. Occasionally, a person will let me know that he or she has no choice but to attend. Some say it as a matter of fact. Others express their displeasure.

Meet Sandy. Sandy was openly upset. The people at her table were noticeably uncomfortable when she shared her story of being forced to attend and what she thought it! As far as what she wanted to get out of the day? She made it very clear that she wanted nothing out of the day. There was a significant shift in the energy of the room as Sandy added her element of discontent.

It's amazing how one person can impact a whole room. Fortune Cookies are like that. They send out messages that are anything but sunny. It seems they are the clouds on a partly cloudy day.

The once sunny, now partly cloudy day continued as we moved into group work. I noted how Sandy's group accomplished less, had fewer discussions, and seemed to be having a lot less fun than the others. At coffee break, I approached Sandy. "How are you doing?" I asked.

She shrugged and responded, "Okay, I guess." It didn't sound okay.

"It seems as if this training, and because you had to be here, isn't something you are enjoying," I said. "I will understand if you wish to leave." My inside voice was saying, Please, please leave.

"No, I don't want to go back to work either," she said.

Darn! said my inside voice. "Did you sign in?" I asked.

"Yeah, why?" She seemed defensive.

"Oh, I was just checking," I said and left it at that. What almost slipped out was my suggestion that she leave and that her leaving would be our little secret. I didn't say that, but I wanted to!

The day continued with my managing the groups so that Sandy worked with a variety of people. On one hand, that strategy worked well because no one small group was impacted for very long. On the other hand, it felt like I was moving around a little storm cloud. Instead of one group getting soaked, everybody got a little rain.

Ever the optimist, I thought that filling out the evaluation form at the end of the day might give Sandy the opportunity to share what she disliked the least about the workshop. Her response to "What did you enjoy most about the workshop?" was "NOTHING!" Her response to "What about the workshop would you improve?" was "NOTHING!" Well, that was that. At least I had an umbrella.

Strategies for Fortune Cookies

Fortune Cookies, when pressed to adjust their behaviour at work, find it difficult to do. If the glass is half empty, it's half empty. Asking them to change their perspective doesn't work. A glass being half full doesn't make sense. When working with a Fortune Cookie, I avoid trying to show them the half-full perspective. I get straight to behaviour and its negative impact. Here are some tasks that I use and approaches that I take to assign them.

Once I have collected information about the exact behaviours that are negatively impacting others, I present that information to this cookie. My intention is to be as objective as possible. By describing behaviour and not personality, I avoid judgement. It is not my place to judge, just to help adjust behaviour.

Our initial discussion involves the cookie's understanding the difference between behaviour and personality.

The Fortune Cookie must increase self-awareness by asking himself or herself the following questions:

How often do I counter someone's opinion with my own?

How often do I talk about what doesn't work, what is wrong with a situation, and use "no" when speaking?

What is my body language like? What is the tone of my voice like when I express my opinion?

What words do I use to describe situations

How do I talk about future events?

I ask the Fortune Cookie to research and determine the differences between an optimist and a pessimist, as well as asking them to define the difference between a pessimist and a realist. The point being that sometimes the glass is indeed half empty; you need a Plan B, and that's just being real. A pessimist would have a Plan B as well. Eventually, the pessimist would conclude that Plan B wouldn't work either.

Once the above terms have been described, I ask the Fortune Cookie to complete the following:

Describe the benefits and drawbacks of each perspective

Identify the place each has in an organization (e.g., useful for..., not useful for...)

The Fortune Cookie needs to develop an awareness of his or her impact on others. As a manager, the Fortune Cookie must understand how he or she sets the tone for the department, team, or organization.

Practice acknowledging others' opinions without commenting on what is wrong with the idea or suggestion.

If You Are Working With or Know a Fortune Cookie

1. Bring an umbrella. It's important to be aware of the Fortune Cookie's impact. Being aware will help you "protect" yourself by not getting sucked into a negative perspective. When in conversation, choose to ignore the negative comments. Continue as if they were not spoken. Don't give the perspective any energy.

2. Avoid countering the Fortune Cookie's perspective. If need be, restate your opinion as your opinion and leave it at that.

3. Remember that we all have reasons for behaving the way we do. You may not understand why the Fortune Cookie has negative messages, but there will be a reason.

4. Don't believe the message.

5. Ask for a solution. If the Fortune Cookie disagrees with a suggestion saying that, "It won't work," ask, "What will work?"

Fortune Cookies may question change but may also question status quo. They may not even stand out as overtly negative, but rather working quietly with their negative magic. Persistent and consistent negative messages identify the Fortune Cookie.

Even though everyone reading this book knows a negative person, it isn't the disproportionate number of Fortune Cookies that is problematic, it's their disproportionate impact. One Fortune Cookie can impact an entire work team ... or workshop!

Why is it so easy to get drawn into the Fortune Cookie's world? Imagine there is a plate of real Fortune Cookies sitting on your desk. You see the edge of a message peeking through the opening of one cookie. Do you open it to read the message? Most of us would. After all, it is a Fortune Cookie. Charles H. Duell was the Commissioner of US patent office in 1899. His comment that "everything that can be invented has been invented" is quite astounding and utterly wrong.[5] Mr. Duell may have been a Fortune Cookie.

5. Dennis Crouch, "Tracing the Quote: Everything that can be Invented has been Invented," PATENTLYO, January 6, 2011. https://patentlyo.com/patent/2011/01/tracing-the-quote-everything-that-can-be-invented-has-been-invented.html

Chapter 12: The Imperial Cookie

Summary of Strengths and Challenges

Strengths:
- Charismatic

Challenges:
- Generally, not competent but proceeds anyway
- Others become distracted by the negative outcomes created by this cookie and forget to remove the source

Imperial Cookies work hard at appearing successful and use their image to help propel them to higher status and success. Imperial Cookies are self-centred and self-serving. The companies they work for are seen as stepping-stones to individual success. There is little loyalty to the company.

Caproni's [6] two managerial types, empty suits and expansive managers, fit the Imperial Cookie category. Empty suits are managers who speak as if they are expert. They are not. They look good

---

6. Caproni, Paula, Management Skills for Everyday Life 3rd Edition (New York, New York) Prentice Hall, 2012)

but lack competency. Expansive managers are ones who have the competencies but are motivated to use their knowledge for self-promotion rather than fulfilling the company's goals.

One day, as I was listening to CBC Radio, I heard the High Tea Bakery was nominated as the best place in Winnipeg to buy cookies. They were famous for the Imperial Cookie. The owner said they sell out daily. I wanted one! I wasn't far from the store, so I drove there immediately. The Imperial Cookie was indeed a fine cookie. With two shortbread biscuits, raspberry jam, and almond icing, I understood how this cookie was such a hit.

The word Imperial brings to mind decadence, power, authority, and importance in a world where great emphasis is placed on ceremony and display. The Imperial Cookie, therefore, is a wonderful category to describe empty suits and expansive managers.

The real Imperial Cookie lives up to its name because it is so delicious. The Imperial Cookie manager lives up to its name through an exaggerated sense of self-importance. They put on quite a show. Well, more of a circus. It's all about them and their being recognized.

In smaller companies, Imperial Cookies are more easily identified and held accountable for their behaviours. Larger companies may be less willing to admit their mistake in selecting such a candidate. By not intervening in poor leadership, companies are vulnerable to an Imperial Cookie's divisive strategies. Imperial Cookies hog the limelight, do not give credit, criticize peers, employees, and even clients or customers, as well as twist events to suit their own needs. The larger the stage, the bigger the show and the greater the damage. One would think that these managers wouldn't last – they can.

Those exposed to Imperial Cookies start to recognize their false fronts and hidden motives. When faced with constant contact, however, something scary happens: a) people become convinced that the Imperial Cookie truly has the skills ("perhaps we are just not seeing them") and b) the superficial behaviours, becoming everyday events, start to appear less extreme. As a result, it becomes acceptable to work with or know the forever-boasting boss.

Imperial Cookies can be mildly annoying, and in many cases, their behaviours are seen as quirks unless they are in a position of leadership. The more powerful the position, the more danger-ous an Imperial becomes. People learn to live with and tolerate bad leadership until the light is shone on the Imperial Cookie. Then what was accepted becomes unacceptable. It is as if the people around the Imperial Cookie have awakened from a bad dream. I believe that there are many political leaders who fall into the Imperial Cookie category. These leaders are not only tough cookies; they are toxic.

I ask one of my university classes to write a one-page summary of how they applied the material from each chapter of our text. One student asked permission to write all twelve summaries about her manager. She was frustrated by working with a leader who frequently boasted about his great leadership skills.

"I can't believe he says these things. He is the furthest thing from a good manager that I can imagine." she said. She went on to describe how he took credit for others' work (including hers) and how she tried to speak with him about her concerns.

"He turned it back on me," she said. "He started listing all the things I was doing wrong and flat out stated that he did nothing to warrant any critical feedback!"

The Imperial Cookie I met was certainly ... uh ... an Imperial Cookie! I had a meeting scheduled with the CEO of a company. The manager of one of the company's divisions was also present. He started speaking, and an hour later he was still speaking! He spoke about his accomplishments and apparently being an expert in almost everything, he had a lot to say. I interrupted a few times, trying to keep the meeting on track. The minute I took a breath, he started speaking again, resulting in one person talking, and two in a coma. I wondered why the director didn't step in and redirect this behaviour. It was not my place to question this or challenge the Imperial Cookie in front of his boss. I found out later that the manager was terminated. Though I don't know how that came about, I suspect the director "woke up."

The Reign of Robert

Robert applied for a senior leadership position in a very large company that I will call Company X. There were many candidates for the position. Most of the candidates were familiar with the industry. Only one candidate had absolutely no experience in the area—Robert. Robert had an impressive resume; Robert got an interview. During the interview, Robert was charismatic and came across as nothing short of brilliant. Certainly, he was not familiar with the industry, but he had new and different (sometimes very different) ideas. What a fresh face to lead the company to further success! What Company X couldn't have foreseen was the train wreck that was about to happen. I did not work with Robert. I was aware, however, of the details.

The reign started with great momentum. People were impressed. Robert's credentials were touted throughout the company. Senior officials were proud, middle managers were excited, and even the frontline workers were excited about someone who wasn't the "same old, same old" leader. The grand old clique was changing! Robert was different. Robert was someone with whom they could identify. Robert would set things straight! Three cheers for Robert! If Robert were a political leader, he would have their votes.

What frontline workers didn't know was that even though they could identify with Robert, Robert could not identify with them. At least Robert did not discriminate. He criticized everyone, frontline workers, clients, peers or even his superiors all equally.

If someone disagreed with Robert, Robert would retaliate. People were subjected to unfair treatment based on unsubstantiated allegations. Punishment was swift. Get on board or get out. What Robert didn't seem to realize was that when he threw the conductor off the train, he was putting everything and everyone in jeopardy. Robert continued to alienate those around him. The train hit a curve.

One by one, people started to question and then doubt Robert's ability to lead the company. A few key colleagues expressed their concern. Robert did not care. How did they know that he didn't care? He said so. The train started to accelerate with no one around to put on the brakes. Others started to doubt. Yet, there remained key colleagues and ever-hopeful employees that stood behind Robert in spite of his bizarre behaviour.

Others questioned the behaviour. Surely something should be done! What company would allow such poor leadership? Surely the company would step in, fire the Imperial Cookie, and get things back on track! You would think so, but sometimes what is obvious to outsiders is missed or rationalized by those caught up in the situation. They exist in a blissful state of denial.

"This can't really be happening, can it?" and "It's not that bad!" muttered senior officials. "Sure, Robert is over the top, a bully, a liar, and is dragging our reputation into the mud," the leaders exclaimed, "But maybe these changes are good." Outside of the company, people saw what was happening - Robert was bad for the company. The train wreck followed. When senior officials finally admitted that Robert could not and should not lead the company, Robert was terminated. What happened to Robert? I never found out for sure. I did hear, however, that he was hired to lead on a much bigger stage. Scary!

Not all Imperial Cookies are as tough as Robert. Not all leave destruction in their leadership wake. Robert was a special combination of an expansive manager (competent in many areas) and an empty suit (not competent in areas that mattered). Roberts are rare, thank goodness. Imperial Cookies are ones whose ambitions are self-centred rather than company-centred. Empty suits show up more often than we think. Perhaps the phrase, "It's hard to get good help these days" came from someone who worked with Imperial Cookies.

Strategies for the Imperial Cookie

Do you see the paradox in the title of this section? If all Imperial Cookies were "Robert-like" then most would not be open to coaching. As noted, however, most Imperial Cookies are not like Robert and still recognize they have not reached perfection. If an Imperial Cookie can see the "what's in it for me" (WIIFM), then coaching would be something to help them succeed. The following exercises may prove of some use to the Imperial Cookie:

1. Stop and listen. Speak less, listen more.
2. Ask others what they need from you.
3. Educate yourself about real leadership. Research. Ask yourself, "Do I emulate these traits?"
4. Speak less, listen more.
5. Count the number of "I's" you use when talking to another person.
6. If someone comes to you for help, don't go on and on about yourself, telling them what you would do, what you have done, how knowledgeable you are in this area, and how lucky they are to learn from you, etc., etc., etc.? (Too much? You wouldn't do this? Remember Robert!)
7. Speak less, listen more.
8. Do you bring conversations back to you and your experiences as opposed to listening and trying to understand others' perspectives?

9. Have you started a conversation only to notice a) people are nodding off, b) people are attempting to leave, c) people look like they are about to faint from boredom, or d) people are staring off into space? If so, you might be an Imperial Cookie.

10. Speak less, listen more.

If You Are Working With or Know an Imperial Cookie

1. Recognize the traits noted in this section and pay attention to them.
2. Do not minimize disrespectful or otherwise unacceptable behaviour.
3. Call their bluff. Imperial Cookies need someone with a proverbial "bigger stick" to send this message.
4. Pin them down, ask "What did you mean by ...?"
5. Ask for specific solutions. If they will make the company great, just how do they propose to do so? What is their plan, specifically?
6. Do not allow deviation from respect, acceptance, equality, and other values of most successful companies.
7. Deliver direct feedback. Be very clear on what is acceptable and what is not. Do not beat around the bush.
8. Monitor their behaviour. Check in with those who work with the Imperial Cookie.
9. Do not allow them to interrupt, put anyone down, or speak negatively about any aspect of the company.
10. Above all remember a most valuable guideline, "If it seems too good to be true, it probably is." And if you meet a "Robert" remember, "If it walks like a duck and talks like a duck, IT'S A DUCK, NOT A SWAN!"

Chapter 13: The Refrigerator Cookie

Summary of Strengths and Challenges

Strengths:
- Steady and thorough worker in the right environment

Challenges:
- Will become impatient, frustrated, and angry when the work environment is too chaotic
- Multi-tasking and responding to out-of-the-box situations are difficult

Refrigerator Cookies are well liked because of their steady and low-key demeanour. Those around them are surprised, therefore, when they become sharp, critical, impatient, and overly analytical. Unlike Ginger Snaps, Refrigerator Cookies don't raise their voices or end up yelling. Rather, these cookies will show they are very upset through obvious disapproval of others and by getting impatient. Little things become big deals. Refrigerator Cookies, having been removed from the perfect conditions of the refrigerated environment, become temperamental. In other words, when the environment becomes too challenging, the element of self-control and the calm, organized approach melts. The cookies have reached their shelf life. This happens all too frequently making Refrigerator Cookies tough.

A Tale of Two Cookies and the Missing Ingredient

The title of this section sounds like a mystery novel. Well, it does contain a bit of a mystery! More on that, later.

I met with two senior leaders in an organization. Though they worked in different departments, supervising very different types of work, each had an employee not meeting performance expectations. Ray worked for one director. Rachel worked for the other. Ray and Rachel did not know each other. Both directors employed succession planning in the process of training individuals into a leadership role. Ray had been selected from his area, Rachel from hers.

The directors relayed similar stories. Both Rachel and Ray showed promise for promotion because each was a steady, hardworking employee. Little conflict surrounded each employee, as both seemed to get along with their colleagues very well. Both accepted the challenge of a supervisory role. It was expected the transition would be smooth. They were both technically competent and seemed to have better than average people skills. Moreover, their teammates seemed excited and pleased to have them promoted. "It was good," one colleague reported, "to have someone who knew the work, be the supervisor." Life was good—in the refrigerator. Being a supervisor, however, requires a different set of skills. Multi-tasking, getting results through others, and working in an unpredictable environment are typical of a supervisory role. Neither Ray nor Rachel was prepared for life outside the controlled environment of being responsible for his and her own performance. They were not prepared for life outside of the refrigerator. Life outside the refrigerator is not cool!

Both directors described each employee as having a "melt down." Each melted down a little differently and each fared differently, as well. Let's look at Ray.

Ray was a very organized person. His workstation was always in order, and due to his organized nature, if anyone needed a document, Ray's computer was a virtual archive. When Ray became a supervisor, he took the time to understand his new responsibilities. There was a new system to organize his new role. Ray started out strong. Everybody seemed pleased. Then the refrigerator door opened. Work became very busy. Ray needed to deal with performance challenges, complex scheduling, multiple vendors, and more meetings in a month than he'd had in six months in his pre-supervisory role.

In order to meet the increasing need to multi-task, Ray started coming in earlier and staying later. The more he tried to become organized, the less time he had to do so. Slowly, Ray's easygoing demeanour was replaced by his being impatient, tense, and short-tempered.

Meanwhile, in another department, Rachel was transitioning to her new role as a supervisor. Rachel was thorough and consistently produced quality work. Now she needed to produce quality work through others. Many people call themselves perfectionists, but Rachel was the epitome of precision and accuracy. When she took on the role of the supervisor, she began to learn the job of each person on her team. She felt she needed to know all the details of all positions in order to be a good supervisor. While she was learning, she wasn't doing the job of a supervisor. Rachel became very stressed. She began to doubt her abilities as a supervisor, and it bothered her—a lot! Learning what everyone did, in detail, was not practical. It was like learning eight new jobs in a very short time frame. It was impossible to do this and her own work at the same time. Later, Rachel admitted that she found delegation very difficult. Rachel became distressed at the pressure and her lack of confidence didn't help. She was outside the refrigerator, and she was melting.

A refrigerator has a controlled environment. Humidity, temperature and even light are regulated. A Refrigerator Cookie has an ingredient that needs refrigeration in order to maintain its integrity. Outside the fridge, that element becomes unstable. As a result, this cookie has a short shelf life.

Ray was becoming increasingly angry and taking it out on those around him. Rachel was becoming increasingly frustrated and was making those around her very uncomfortable. Both supervisors needed to find that mysterious, missing ingredient that would allow them to handle life outside of the refrigerator. Rachel found it; Ray did not.

Coaching with Ray involved getting back to the basics. He was advised that if he became frustrated, he should walk away from a situation. He must not show his frustration to his direct reports. Unfortunately, as many times as Ray tried, Ray failed. He expressed frustration when an employee did not have the report he had requested. He expressed frustration when others didn't seem to understand how to analyze data from the new system. He didn't understand why he, as he expressed, "had to think for everyone who reported to him."

By the end of the probation period, Ray and the director decided the job was not for him. Under stress, his well-meaning intentions went flying out the window. He could not control situations that weren't orderly or predictable. Management is anything but predictable. When it feels like you're juggling three or four balls in the air while walking on a tightrope without a net, you know you are in management. Ray was given a different position within the organization that did not involve supervision. He was much happier, the organization (especially HR) was much happier, and his former direct reports, when he met up with them, were a little less angry every day.

Rachel's journey had different results. She showed up at our initial meeting with some degree of trepidation. She was cautious about all matters, preferring to size up the situation, analyze it, and then decide how to respond. The methodical approach was replaced with sudden reactions. A minor incident became a big deal as she became increasingly reactive. She was outside the refrigerator and coming to the end of her shelf life! When we met, I noticed, by the way in which Rachel talked, that she cared about her job, her future, and her direct reports. She wanted to do the job right, and she was making mistakes. She confessed she wasn't used to making mistakes and it was unnerving. She seemed to relax during our session, and it made a difference. She was less focused on all the things she was doing wrong and became more focused on what she needed to change in order to succeed as a supervisor. We started with baby steps.

At the end of our first session, I gave Rachel some homework. It involved filling out a personality profile assessment. I asked her to pay attention to the description of what happens to her personality type under stress. She asked me why. I explained that I wanted her to understand that there was a pattern to her behaviour as she moved from feeling capable to being lost in chaos. If she could identify a pattern, then she could intervene before she started to melt. In other words, I wanted her to cool down without having to go back into the refrigerator. I also asked her to walk away from any incident where she was becoming frustrated. She asked me, "How?" We brainstormed and came up with a few options. She selected the one she thought would be most effective. I set up our next appointment for later that week.

"What will we be doing?" she asked. "Reviewing the profile and seeing if the option you selected, worked," I replied.

From that point on, there was a pattern to her learning. It involved frequent use of the words: why, what, how, when, what if, what about, how would I, and so on. Rachel was excellent at ensuring she understood. She completed her homework and took one baby step at a time. It took much less time than one might have guessed for Rachel to keep her cool even out of the refrigerator. What was the mystery ingredient? Why was she able to control her meltdowns, while Ray could not?

Rachel added an ingredient that stabilized her need for control and perfect organization. She increased her self-regulation. By applying her thorough and methodical approach to herself, she was able to identify when she started to get upset and why. She learned to employ different strategies to cope with getting upset and got back to being centred. She was much more flexible than I gave her credit for in our first meeting. She learned about her style, its strengths, and its challenges. She felt less isolated, and by controlling what she learned and how much, she reduced her stress by getting back a sense of control.

Rachel was able to learn self-control and thus did not need the refrigerator. Ray was not able to self-regulate. Ray's strategy was focused on "I'm not going to get mad," so consequently he did. Even though our exercises addressed what to do (walk away), he was focused on suppressing the anger. I've never been successful with that strategy. Ray wasn't either. Rachel's strategy was focused on "How do I stay calm?" These are two vastly different approaches. One focuses on anger and the other on being calm. One involves suppression of a strong reaction; the other involves replacing the reaction with a response.

Strategies for the Refrigerator Cookie

"Chill out" might seem rather glib but this tough cookie has a daunting challenge. It must be able to let go of a controlled environment by practicing self-control in the chaotic world of management.

Practice stress management techniques.

Self-regulation is part of managing stress, and it is also a fundamental ingredient in emotional intelligence (EI). Therefore, a strategy essential for a Refrigerator Cookie is to increase her or his emotional quotient (EQ).

If You Are Working With or Know a Refrigerator Cookie

Since self-regulation is something only the Refrigerator Cookie can do for him or herself, strategies for others working with or knowing this cookie are not as effective, however...

If you can, assist the Refrigerator Cookie by staying calm and patient, even when he or she appears upset.

In the world of the Refrigerator Cookie, a sudden change in a presenting problem can have a significant impact, so give clear directions.

Give the Refrigerator Cookie time to learn new tasks and allow them to learn their jobs in stages. By doing so, they build confidence and a feeling of control as they transition to a new position.

Provide leadership and emotional intelligence coaching at the beginning of the transition, for three months followed by a break of three months, and finally by coaching for an additional three months.

Management and supervision are very different than working in your own job. Leading others requires different skills, multitasking being just one. Some people promoted to supervision are not given the training and coaching to transition successfully. Coaching is especially important for Refrigerator Cookies if you want them to succeed. Coaching allows them to slowly add the mystery ingredient of self-regulation.

Chapter 14: The Shortbread Cookie

Summary of Strengths and Challenges

Strengths:
- Can be the finest and most endurable cookie of them all, honouring tradition as well as staying current

Challenges:
- It's either a good shortbread cookie or it isn't
- Tries to solve long-term problems with short-term solutions

Nessie, the Highlands, Inverness, Runrig, good friends, and shortbread. Yes, I am speaking of Scotland, its beauty, its music, and its famous cookie—the shortbread cookie. I have fond memories of Scotland. I walked around Inverness with a wonderful local artist, Margaret. We visited various shops and I tasted real shortbread. She showed me how to use a shortbread mold so that I had a cookie as large as a pie and in the shape of a thistle. It was pretty and pretty delicious. Shortbread cookies are my all-time favourite treat. I like shortbread even more than chocolate, and that says a lot. How strange it is, therefore, that the Shortbread cookie should be the cookie that tests my patience above all others.

Consider how a shortbread cookie is made. It uses a few simple ingredients, yet it seems difficult to get everything just right to create a firm but mouth-watering sweet. Regardless of the variety of the ratio, only the finest ingredients turn out the finest cookies. Use margarine instead of butter, and you don't have the same cookie. Margarine is easier and often at hand whereas butter may take a bit more effort to get it just right to put into the mix.

As mentioned, Shortbread cookies can represent an individual or a company. It represents how quickly and how frequently a company can self-sabotage, or an individual can ruin a department by being incredibly short-sighted and dense. The term "cut the fat," in an organization, takes on a whole different meaning in the world of tough cookies. Removing top performers because they are too expensive is akin to swapping margarine for butter. Leaving positions vacant is a similar error. If you have a good mix and are producing a good product, don't change the recipe just because it's cheaper.

The ingredients to shortbread are not exotic: fat, flour, and sugar. The ingredients to successful leadership are not complicated. You need good ingredients in leadership and in shortbread. The reality, however, is that the good ingredients are often passed over for what is handy. You can't create a good cookie with missing or poor ingredients. You cannot have a successful company with missing or poor leadership.

The Shortbread cookie represents short-sightedness. A person or a company creates long-term pain for short-term gain. In real life, it represents a person who is focused on solving the immediate problem or challenge in such a way that creates greater problems later. But later is later for the Shortbread cookie and later doesn't matter. Shortbread cookies are companies that fail to invest in long-term employee development and managers who focus on getting the immediate results even though it stresses staff and drives top performers away.

How to Ruin a Company in a Year or Less

This story isn't about one person; it's about a company. The company became one big tough cookie. Let's look at the "before" picture.

- Diverse group of employees with established culture of good customer service
- Long-term employees
- Many smiles
- Warm and welcoming atmosphere
- Going above and beyond for service
- Staff knew their long-term clients
- Accommodations were made for staff facing difficulties or life challenges
- As shift work was required, there was great flexibility and staff were allowed to participate in shift changes and preferences
- Staff supported each other; when there were unpredicted gaps of service, everyone who could filled in the gaps
- Employees felt valued by management and owners of the company
- Employees considered themselves a close-knit team where everyone mattered, equally

As with life, nothing stays the same. The leadership changed. The leadership looked at the company's bottom line and decided it could be more profitable. The new owners wanted a better return on their investment, and they wanted it quick. Changes were implemented, without consultation or any employee input. Very suddenly an "us/them" state emerged. There were rumblings and rumours about what was going to happen to the company and its staff. Enter a new manager, hired by "them" to get this company out of its low-profit state to an acceptable return on investment.

The new manager was very much in tune with intent of the new owners. He oversaw the transition to a new state of business. If he was a shortbread baker, he would be the type to open the fridge and grab the margarine because it was cheaper, easier to work with, and very, very handy. Some of the strategies that went into this company's becoming tough were as follows:

Employees were scrutinized and written up on every infraction. What was acceptable before now became part of disciplinary action.

- Long-term and high-performing employees left in droves.
- Some employees were terminated for their lack of performance yet went on to other, similar organizations only to be heralded as top performers. In one case, a manager of this tough cookie company faced retaliation for speaking out against how the employees were being treated. She was fired. Yet within months she was promoted to management in a similar company. I believe she is still there, doing the fine job she had always done.
- Employees reported "sticking it out" because they were close to retirement; they were afraid they might not find another job and couldn't afford to take the chance, or because they felt a certain loyalty to the company regardless of its change in ownership.
- Remaining staff survived on a diet of rumours, fear of retaliation, and more "fat cutting."

A year or so later the results were as follows:
- Connections with local community groups were strained.
- Employees came and went.

- There were a lot of hard feelings as employees left. One employee was known for bringing in fancy pens that she had decorated to cheer up the remaining staff. When she left, she was asked to leave them behind because they were company property. They weren't. She said being treated as a thief after many years of service was hurtful. She gave me a pen. It still serves as a reminder of what can happen with the use of lesser ingredients.
- One employee asked for an exit interview. She wanted to let the new owners know how staff were being treated. "They" never responded to the request.
- The company did not survive in its current state. It changed its service and morphed into something that would provide a more stable funding source. The once-thriving business was no more.

Cut the Fat, Kill the Cookie

The company described above is not unlike many that seek to improve the bottom line while demoralizing and destroying its human resource. Even though research proves that, when companies invest in their human capital, the payoff is great. Happy employees work harder, work better, and will work longer than necessary for a company that shows it cares. The company is represented by each of its leaders, so those who lead must understand this very simple formula: investing in human capital brings increased profit. Additionally, I find tough cookie companies amazingly dense and short-sighted when they take the approach that short-term gain in a financial bottom line is a wise business decision. At best, they will create an average company with above average problems and lose financially in the long run.

One senior leader of an organization relayed a strategy not only to "cut the fat" but also replace long-term employees with younger employees who had fresh new ideas. It seems that the organization didn't realize that all employees will want the same things, respect, and appreciation. If it was not willing to establish a culture of appreciation and engage current employees, then the same problems will arise. They will again be faced with poor performance and an exodus of talent. Replacing staff is much more expensive than developing current employees.

There are so many companies that have cut resources, left positions unfilled, and have expected employees to do double duty. These companies have repeatedly replaced the building of trust with the demanding of results and subsequently ensure a hierarchy where one is very clear where the bottom of the corporate ladder is. I find it most perplexing when such an organization turns to a consultant to improve morale and discover why employees lack motivation. Talent does not stay where there is such a short-sighted approach. One participant, in one of my workshops, asked, "What if you train your employees and they leave?" To which another participant replied, "What if you don't and they stay?" That about sums it up!

Strategies for the Shortbread Tough Cookie

I like fantasy, but I am under no illusion that companies seeking the short-term gain will read this and experience an epiphany that sounds something like this: "Quick, someone get us some butter! We've been going about this all wrong! We need to do something different! These are the strategies we must use." Nevertheless, the following:

- Invest in our people; train and coach them for further development aligned with our new direction.
- Get them engaged; listen to them.
- Utilize their strengths and experience to mobilize existing resources.

- Ensure our leaders have the training and support to create a positive workplace.
- Evaluate our leaders as much as we have them evaluate their employees.
- Hold all leaders accountable
- Give employees the resources they need to do the work that's expected of them.
- Build trust.
- Demonstrate that we are all a part of the same team; de-emphasize the hierarchy.
- Share a clear vision.
- Establish values and ensure all leaders model those employees.
- Ensure our leaders are trained in and demonstrate the five practices of exemplary leadership described in The Leadership Challenge[7]:
  1. Model the way
  2. Inspire a shared vision
  3. Challenge the process
  4. Enable others to act
  5. Encourage the heart
- Coach our leaders to coach others.
- Hold our leaders accountable to treat performance challenges as opportunities for development through effective feedback skills.
- Ensure we recognize and reward our employees in meaningful ways.
- Hold performance reviews, have employees evaluate their own performance, and use theirs as comparison to their managers' evaluations of their performance.
- Create learning plans.

---

7. Kouzes & Posner, The Leadership Challenge.

If You Are Working for a Shortbread Company or Individual

- Quit. Look for another job where finer ingredients are used. They are out there and are looking for employees like you!

Chapter 15: The Double Chocolate Chunk Macadamia Nut Cookie

Summary of Strengths and Challenges

Strengths:
- They are sweet

Challenges:
- They are sweet

Once upon a time, there was a box of assorted cookies that were called to action. They were needed at a very important business meeting. They were the afternoon treats. The assorted cookies were so excited. They were a diverse group. There were chocolate chip cookies, peanut butter cookies, finger cookies with icing (three different colours of icing, no less), mud pies (a company favourite), and those little cookies with icing between two chocolate biscuits. This group of cookies endorsed their diversity so thoroughly that even the sugar-free cookies and the digestive biscuits were a part of the team. Those cookies didn't have to face the stigma of not having real sugar or having a name with the word "digestive" in it.

The afternoon was upon them. Excited, they were removed from the box. Suddenly something went wrong. Other cookies were already out on a separate tray. A nice, shiny-like-silver type of tray sat in their place! Wait a minute! That was their tray! It was the same one the company had used for all their meetings. It was always in the same place in the centre of the table closest to the coffee and tea. It was tradition! Who were these new cookies? Where did they come from? What were they like? Why were people standing around in awe of them? As the hands reaching for those cookies moved away, the other cookies saw for themselves what was happening, and they were shocked.

Right there beside them was a new type of cookie! It was chocolate; it had chocolate chunks, and macadamia nuts! There were so many cookies it was practically an army! How did this happen? There was no memo that a new cookie would be joining the team. The chocolate chip started to feel inferior against the chunks of dark chocolate. The sugar-free cookie felt less authentic, and the digestive biscuit seemed to hide under the peanut butter. The peanut butter cookie, perhaps, took it the hardest. So many people would not allow him in the building. He was made with peanuts! Now he was being placed beside the rich and decadent macadamia nut! The icing on the finger cookies began to melt ever so slightly.

The tray of double chocolate chunk macadamia nut cookies disappeared. A few people grumbled, "Darn, they're all gone! I guess a chocolate chip will have to do!"

"Too bad," another person said. "They were delicious!"

The mud pie cookies were offended.

"It's probably going to spike my blood sugar, but I had to have one!" another person admitted.

The sugar-free cookie was devastated.

"I'll bet we are going to get really sleepy this afternoon after this," the chair of the meeting chuckled.

"Serves you right," mumbled the digestive cookie.

Not one person selected the finger cookies with the decorative icing. "I guess I couldn't keep it together," admitted the finger cookie. "Now, I've got icing all over everything!" Only the little cookies with the icing between two chocolate biscuits were unaffected.

"How come you're so calm?" asked the other cookies, almost in unison.

"Look at the beverages," one of the calm cookies instructed. "No milk."

Such is the story of our tough cookie, the Double Chocolate Chunk Macadamia Nut cookie (DCCMN). It's a special cookie, and that's part of the problem.

Strategies for the DCCMN

Identifying oneself as a DCCMN is almost impossible – almost. One "double-chocolate flag" would be your frequent use of a phrase such as, "That's just the way I am!". Notice the exclamation mark? That's the difference between a descriptive statement of self and a firmly stated excuse for not wanting to adjust behaviour. The following are strategies to raise your awareness:

1. If there has been a pattern of people backing off or being offended by something you have done or said, pay attention. Remember, it will be extremely difficult for people to give you the feedback you will request. It is hard to describe the feeling of being overshadowed without its coming across as a lack of confidence, competition, or even petty.

2. When you are tired or stressed, this is an important time to check how you are behaving and how the other people around you are doing.

3. Occasionally, inconvenience yourself to address the needs of others.

If You Are Working With or Know a DCCMN

1. Establish clear boundaries, not between you and this tough cookie, but for yourself entirely. For example, focus on your own choices, on what you will and will not accept.
2. Don't compete; don't even try.
3. Set rules through your own assertive behaviour. You don't need to say anything, necessarily, but your actions must be assertive, not passive or aggressive. If you act aggressively and show anger and frustration, the tough DCCMN will not understand how or why you got to this point. If you act passively, the DCCMN will unknowingly takeover situations such as meetings, presentations, and even small group interaction. Strangely enough, at times, the DCCMN may take over a situation under the guise of helping you.
4. Walk away when you need to in order to gain perspective.

Chapter 16: The Chocolate Puff

A Summary of Strengths and Challenges

Strengths:
- Loyal
- Will go the distance to help others

Challenges:
- Their direct, practical approach can come across as angry and judgmental resulting in others feeling uncomfortable or fearful of them

There are endearing memories from my childhood. Strangely a lot of them are about food, which might explain the nature of this book. I remember the brown bag of french fries Dad would bring home, my trying to make my own version of salt and vinegar chips by dumping vinegar into the bag, and ... Ok, cookies. My favourite cookie was the Chocolate Puff. It had a firm wafer crumb base with a dollop of jam in the middle covered by a chocolate-crusted marshmallow. They are still in the stores today. (In my local grocery store ... four aisles over, halfway down the aisle, on the left, second shelf!) It's a classic.

The Art of Eating a Chocolate Puff

This cookie provides variety. There is a base, a sweet jam, a soft marshmallow, and chocolate. All seriously good parts of a seriously good cookie!

The other cookies we have examined are consistent in texture. That is, when you bite into an oatmeal raisin for example, there is no surprise inside. It is an oatmeal raisin, through and through. You know what to expect. Even the Imperial Cookie is not surprising in this sense. You see quite plainly that there is a filling between the two biscuits. The Chocolate Puff, however, has surprises inside in the form of the soft interior, the jam and the delicious base.

The Chocolate Puff, because its interior is different from its exterior, is fun to eat. In fact, it's an art! Did you know there are life lessons to be learned by eating a Chocolate Puff? I'm guessing that hasn't crossed your mind. The lessons will help us with human Chocolate Puff tough cookies:

1. Just pick it up and bite into it.
   a. Advantage – You get to discover all of the elements quickly.
   b. Disadvantage – It can be messy with bits of chocolate and crumbs falling everywhere.
   c. The lesson – if you are going to just bite it, be prepared for a little mess.
   d. In human terms, don't attack or you will wind up with a mess.
2. Crack the chocolate in many places with a spoon.

    a. Advantage – you will have less mess since the now-small chocolate pieces will stick to the marshmallow. The base doesn't crumble.

    b. Disadvantage – if you hit too hard, you could knock off big chunks of the chocolate coating and ... you have a mess.

    c. Lesson – don't hit too hard or you will have a mess.

    d. In human terms, don't over react to their communication style.

3. Gently press on the chocolate surface, as if you were lightly knocking on a door. Take the chocolate pieces off one by one and enjoy the chocolate while uncovering the soft interior.

    a. Advantage – less messy.

    b. Disadvantage – it takes patience.

    c. Lesson – You get to see the whole marshmallow.

    d. In human terms, if you spend the time you can turn the tough exterior into a soft exterior.

The Chocolate Puff Cookie

Just like the real cookies, the human Chocolate Puff Cookie is different inside than what is seen on the outside. What you see is not all of what you get. You see a hard surface but find out there is a soft interior. You need to take the time, however, to get to know them.

The Chocolate Puff Cookie is not uncommon. These are the people who appear tough. The exterior is firm but not rock solid. They are not mean, rude, or overbearing. They can be, but generally exhibit a quieter firmness. It might come across as aloof, perhaps unpredictable since their "inside" is covered up. Others tend to be wary of or uncomfortable around them. As a result, others attribute more negative characteristics to them than what the chocolate puffs actually display. If you get the opportunity to know them and establish interpersonal trust, however, you will find they are very compassionate and caring people on the inside. Once you see this, you are seeing the interior. Once you get to the interior, you have the benefit of enjoying the "jam." In human terms, you will have found yourself a true and loyal friend.

It was Paul and Paulette

I would like to describe two tough cookies: one male and one female. Why? There is a stereotype that tough is male and soft is female. Of course, like all stereotypes, this is not accurate. Chocolate Puff Cookies are equally common among females and males.

Paul was a man of selected speech. Paul did not get involved in chit-chat (man of few words), but he could converse at length with someone about a shared interest (selected speech). Paul was not a client but was a colleague and friend. I was finished high school and wanted a job close to home. I began working as a teacher's aide in a nearby community. I was to be an aide for two teachers. One was openly friendly while the other was polite but with an air of distance.

My first morning went well and the afternoon was spent with the less openly friendly Paul. At the completion of each class, we talked about my duties. This repeated itself daily. Near the end of the first week, Paul asked me how I was doing. I relayed my excitement and appreciation for job. Then Paul said something quite interesting. "You are not at all what I expected." Of course, I asked him what he meant. "Well, a few people mentioned they knew you and described you as very outgoing. I was afraid I was going to have to work with a very "hyper" individual, which I would find very annoying." Now you would think I'd be upset by that description, but I was not. I saw how the children loved this teacher and I saw his quiet kindness in return. That was the person I related to and was not disturbed by his direct approach. As a result, working with Paul was a pleasure, and I always got the feeling that should I ever need help in any way, he was the type of person who would be there. Unfortunately, for every one that sees past the exterior, there are just as many who do not.

Flash forward. Paulette was a client. I was hired to provide training for her department and executive coaching for her as a new leader. Paulette was a direct person. She was promoted to supervisor because of her performance in her previous position. She was technically proficient, and there was no indication that she lacked the interpersonal skills to be a supervisor. She was direct but not abrasive … yet.

I was asked to coach Paulette because she had done surprisingly poorly in her 360-degree feedback. Her team's rating was, in fact, terrible. As I got to know Paulette, it was obvious that she was used to doing things her way and telling others what to do. Her directions to others (correcting errors, pointing out shortfalls, etc.) were correct but her focus was flawed. Her drive to have zero errors in production led to her being seen as a taskmaster. That's all they saw because that was all she showed them.

As we worked together, it was obvious that being a taskmaster was not her natural style. She too was bothered by the lack of rapport. She was not a Ginger Snap, but a Chocolate Puff. Her exterior was tough due to the pressure of the new position and its accompanying stress. There is one thing about a Chocolate Puff that you might not be aware of—if it sits out too long in the wrong conditions (out of its package) it dries up. The chocolate doesn't dry up; the marshmallow does. If you bite into a stale Chocolate Puff, the marshmallow is like leather. It is not soft, but it is not solid either. It is not tasty. And the jam is chewy.

Paulette had was out of her element. The soft interior was getting tougher. She was becoming a "tougher" cookie. She was on the verge of losing her job. Fortunately, Paulette's natural style was a firm (not hard) exterior with a soft and caring interior. Coaching reduced some of the stress, allowing her to show more of her relationship-oriented traits. All in all, her team was pleasantly but cautiously surprised when Paulette changed how she communicated with them. Paulette felt better and eventually developed a positive rapport with her team members. She kept her job.

If you are a Chocolate Puff

1. Give people the opportunity to know you.
2. If a person stumbles by judging you and then realizes they are wrong, allow and accept an apology.
3. "Crack up" a few times. Show the lighter, more vulnerable you.

If You Are Working With or Know a Chocolate Puff

There are clear strategies for those who work with or know a Chocolate Puff. It's not a long journey to get to the soft interior and the reward of knowing someone who will be a fierce supporter, be it a friend or colleague, is truly a gift worth earning. Take direction from eating the real Chocolate Puff Cookie.

1. If you approach the Puff and react only to the exterior, then crusty is what you will get. If you try to push them, they will push back with greater strength. If you don't get to know them, their soft interior will turn to leather. There's no going back. There is no way to return the stale cookie to its fresh state. The best that you can hope for is cool, distant, and minimal communication.
2. Take your time to get to know this person. Don't judge them according to your standards. Wait, listen, and learn. Look for the traits of compassion, caring, and being supportive

of others. These traits are not hidden. They are not under a hard shell. It takes only a little nudging to connect with the heart of the Chocolate Puff. Look for it, focus on it, relate to it, and you will reap the benefits of a supportive colleague, supportive supervisor, or a loyal friend.

Chapter 17: The Sugar Cookie

Summary of Strengths and Challenges

Strengths:
- Sweet

Challenges:
- Unyielding
- Unforgiving

Four cookies walk into a restaurant: a Hermit, a Chocolate Puff, a Ginger Snap and a Sugar Cookie. They sit in a booth in a far corner of the room, away from the kitchen. The Sugar Cookie asks, "Hey, have you read the book called Soft Skills for Tough Cookies?"

"I don't have time to read!" said the Ginger Snap.

"No," said the Chocolate Puff.

The Hermit Cookie looked away.

"Well," began the Sugar Cookie and it looked across the table, "According to the book, you are a Ginger Snap. And you," shifting its attention to the cookie sitting beside the Ginger Snap, "are a Chocolate Puff."

Before the Sugar Cookie could continue, the Ginger snapped, "I'm not a Ginger Snap!"

"Oh no?" questioned the Chocolate Puff. "You snap all the time! Besides what's wrong with being a Ginger Snap? At least you aren't called a Puff!"

The Puff looked across at the Sugar Cookie. "I am not soft inside, by the way."

"Well, I'm not happy either," admitted the Sugar Cookie, "I'm a plain old Sugar Cookie; nothing exciting there."

"I don't snap!" the Ginger Snap insisted.

"My shell is rock solid," said the Puff.

The Hermit Cookie looked away.

"We all can be tough cookies, according to this book," continued the Sugar Cookie.

"How so?" the Chocolate Puff and the Ginger Snap asked in unison.

"Well you," said the Sugar Cookie, pointing to the Ginger Snap, "have an underlying heat..."

"I DO NOT," interrupted the Ginger Snap. People glanced their way.

"What about me?" asked the Puff. "How am I tough?"

"Apparently, if not treated right, your soft interior can become dried up and get tough and leathery" responded the Sugar Cookie.

"Ah, tough," said the Puff. "I am indeed very tough."

The Hermit Cookie remained silent.

"And you?" asked the Puff, "What makes you tough?"

"Well, apparently I'm a little different," the Sugar Cookie explained. "I don't seem like a tough cookie to others because I'm nice."

"Oh, really?" replied the Puff, with no attempt to hide the sarcasm.

"And I'm NOT?" The Ginger Snap was becoming unhinged.

The Hermit Cookie got up and left. There was an uncomfortable silence.

"Let's go," said the Ginger Snap. "The coffee here is crumby."

The Sugar Cookie in this scenario interacted well, given the circumstance. It remained sweet. Sugar Cookies are like that. People wouldn't identify them as difficult—tough or otherwise. They are seen as nice people who are genuinely nice. So, when would a Sugar Cookie become a tough cookie?

Let's consider the real Sugar Cookie's composition and how it describes the human Sugar Cookie.

THE REAL SUGAR COOKIE	THE HUMAN SUGAR COOKIE
The cookie is made of sugar, and it has sugar on the outside.	The person is genuinely nice and appears nice to others.
They are basic but with fancy edges.	Being nice does not mean they are quiet, passive individuals. They can have flair, be introverted or extroverted.
They can be covered with coloured sugar or have sprinkles on top; often used to mark occasions such Christmas or Valentines.	They tend to be very adaptable when communicating with others. Focusing on other people, they are able to adjust their communication style to fit into different circumstances and different people.
They are plain but functional. When you think cookie, you think sweet. These cookies are simply... sweet.	They are very good at accepting even the most difficult traits in other people. Their strength lies in being able to accommodate others.

THE REAL SUGAR COOKIE	THE HUMAN SUGAR COOKIE
They are the cookies that seem to be there constantly. They've been around a long time.	In the workplace, they are the standby, go-to person. They can do their job with little supervision since seeking harmony with others allows them to work more effectively.
They are a treat. I remember the school Christmas parties and the community showers, teas, or church luncheons that inevitably had Sugar Cookies. Although basic, they were considered pretty fancy cookies when I was young.	They are a treat in the work environment. They tend to be supportive, friendly, and seem to go out of their way to make others feel good. People trust them.
They may be passed over because of their simplicity in favour of more fancy cookies.	People may tend to take them for granted or repay their being nice with harshness, criticism, or may just dismiss. People may mistake niceness for weakness and unconsciously (or consciously) take advantage of them. This is unfortunate as this is what turns the Sugar Cookie into a tough cookie.
THE REAL SUGAR COOKIE	
If the sugar is over-processed, the sugar is no longer workable. If it burns, it is useless, and there is no way to change that.	It takes a long time for the person to become intolerant. If pushed too far, however, they will shut down, shut you out, and because there is no going back, become one of the toughest cookies of all.

A friend once described herself as being nice and often described as sweet. She pointed out, however, "If someone does not treat me well or tries to walk over me, then I am not so sweet. I have my limits, and if someone pushes me beyond those limits, there is no going back."

Managers who are Sugar Cookies are more relationship-oriented. They would rather get along and would like others to do the same. Sugar Cookie managers will want employees to like them. In order to achieve harmony in the environment, these managers may let tasks and performance slide for a while. If there is a conflict among staff members, they will try to settle things down and encourage cooperation, perhaps without even dealing with the source of the conflict.

If being taken advantage of, Sugar Cookies build up resentment. They become critical of others, even about things that they have ignored in the past. Their being critical is a red flag for others. It is a sign of heat's being applied.

The Sugar Cookie is tough not only because of what happens when too much "heat" of disregard is applied, but also because one doesn't know when the proverbial "line" has been crossed. There is not much indication (if any) that the sugar has turned to hard candy. As Esther the baker said, "There's no going back after that!"

Being Burnt: The Point of No Return

Sugar Cookies have one thing in common. They can identify the one incident that took them to the point of no return. It may have been a seemingly innocent comment or a not so well-intended criticism, but it became the tipping point. In an instant, the sugar is burned. Getting to this point, however, was the result of heat's building up over a period of time. Others will see a change, but probably won't know the reason why. They will identify the comment that burnt the cookie but won't give it due importance and minimize the cookie's reaction, which only further solidifies the burnt sugar. You don't need to walk on eggshells; just pay attention because the Sugar Cookie will give you plenty of indication of displeasure. They do it in a nice way so people rarely see it happening until it is too late.

If you are a Sugar Cookie

The Sugar Cookie works hard at a very difficult task—being nice. It takes energy and hard work to be accepting, flexible, and tolerant. There are ways to help you from getting burnt.

- Ensure you do not allow your acceptance and support of others to take away from your own needs. Staying assertive is essential.
- Communicate your needs before things get too hot.
- Realize the difference between supportive and enabling. You can help them and support them, but you can't breathe for them.
- Know that it's okay to argue. A certain degree of low-level conflict can clear the air.
- Understand that a disagreement does not mean the end of a relationship. It's important to disagree respectfully.
- Don't allow your affability to accept others' negative behaviour.
- Consider being the thermostat and not the thermometer. When you take care of your own needs, you have greater control over yourself and your work environment. This allows you to minimize reaction and "set the temperature" you where you would like it.
- Remember that although you will go out of your way to help others, the same is not guaranteed in return.

If You Are Working With or Know a Sugar Cookie

- Above all, do not assume their being nice means they are weak.
- Notice your impact on them. The Sugar Cookie is not likely to tell you that their feelings are being hurt or that your actions are seen as rude or insensitive. There is an expectation you will catch this. After all, they do.
- Pay attention to the signs of fatigue or stress. Noticing such and stepping in to help the cookie without being told to is key to a good relationship with the Sugar Cookie.
- If they are the helpful type, don't drain them. Don't continue to ask them for help, or "go to the well" too often.

Chapter 18: Cookie Dough

Summary of Strengths and Challenges

Strengths:

- Potential to be one of the most popular cookies ever

Challenges:

- May get gobbled up by stress and circumstance before ever becoming a cookie

The Amazing Coincidence

My middle name is Ruth, and I am writing about cookies. One of the most popular cookies of all time, the chocolate chip cookie was "invented" by Ruth Graves Wakefield. Is this a coincidence perhaps? I think not! Okay, maybe it is. Back to Mrs. Wakefield.

Mrs. Wakefield, a dietician and food lecturer, prepared food for the Toll House Inn in Massachusetts. The popular story purports that, in 1930, she was preparing a traditional cookie that required chocolate, specifically baking chocolate. She did not have any left, and so she cut up Nestlé semi-sweet chocolate that had been given to her by Andrew Nestlé of the Nestlé Company. The chocolate did not melt entirely but stayed as chunks of small chocolates. People loved it, and the rest is history.[8] Other sources state that the switch of ingredients was deliberate.[9] Regardless, the famous chocolate chip cookie arrived.

When I spoke to people about the different types of cookies I was using for this book, a frequent response was, "What? No chocolate chip cookie? That's the most famous cookie of them all. You can't have a tray of cookies and not find a chocolate chip cookie among them." Chocolate chip cookies are a staple, a tradition, and as central to the cookie world as Ruth is to my name. (Coincidence again?) Nonetheless, the chocolate chip cookie is popular. In fact, "half of all home baked cookies are chocolate chip."[10] The Chocolate Chip cookie is the official cookie of Massachusetts.[11] That's pretty sweet.

The dough for chocolate chip cookies is also popular. Now, special dough is made and used in ice cream, becoming a standard in ice cream flavours.[12] Eating raw cookie dough is not recommended even though, as children, stealing some out of the cookie bowl was practically a rite of passage. Today, however, people and companies have created a safe, edible version. Nonetheless, cookie dough is just that—the chocolate chip cookie ingredients

8. Kate Krake, "The Accidental Invention of the Chocolate Chip Cookie," Today I Found Out, March 15, 2013. http://www.todayifoundout.com/index.php/2013/03/the-accidental-invention-of-the-chocolate-chip-cookie/

9. "Chocolate chip cookie," Wikipedia. https://en.wikipedia.org/wiki/Chocolate_chip_cookie Accessed October 26, 2018.

10. "5 Facts About Chocolate Chip Cookies You Probably Didn't Know," Flipping Good Cookies, March 2012. http://blog.flippingoodcookies.com/2012/03/5-facts-about-chocolate-chip-cookies-you-probably-didnt-know/

11. "Cookie Candidates: Pennsylvania State Cookie (proposed)," State Symbols USA. https://statesymbolsusa.org/symbol-official-item/pennsylvania/state-food-agriculture-symbol/chocolate-chip-cookie Accessed October 26, 2018.

12. Nicole Perry, "How Ben & Jerry's Invented Chocolate Chip Cookie Dough Ice Cream," POPSUGAR, April 4, 2015. http://www.popsugar.com/food/Who-Invented-Chocolate-Chip-Cookie-Dough-Ice-Cream-37167903

mixed together and not subjected to heat. Let's take a look at Cookie Dough.

THE AMAZING COINCIDENCE OF COOKIE DOUGH AND THE COOKIE DOUGH MANAGER		
Cookie Dough	Cookie Dough Human	Why the Cookie Dough Manager is a tough cookie
• Is popular	• Is popular	• Being nice may make you popular but it doesn't earn you respect
• If eaten in its unmodified form, it may make you sick	• Some new managers are not able to learn the skills it takes to be an effective supervisor	• If you do not learn and deploy effective supervisory skills, you can become as toxic as any other type of tough cookie
• Will not become a cookie if eaten before it's cooked	• Will not become an effective supervisor if you can't stand the heat	• Leading others requires making some tough decisions. If you are unable to take decisive action (subject yourself to heat), you will not become a successful manager

THE AMAZING COINCIDENCE OF COOKIE DOUGH AND THE COOKIE DOUGH MANAGER		
• Is the beginning of a very popular cookie but needs some baking to harden and shape it	• Is the beginning of one of the most effective managers because people skills are already developed	• If you are not hardened by learning the skills of task behaviour, you will not be shaped into a cookie (effective manager) and forever remain only Cookie Dough, which may be sweet but is not manager material.

Taken to the extreme, the Cookie Dough manager becomes too flexible and gets caught up with employees being friends rather than exercising the role of a firm but fair authority figure. John Maxwell, in his book, The 21 Irrefutable Laws of Leadership: Follow Them and People Will Follow You, says the following, "If you need people, you can't lead people." He went on to explain that if you need people to bolster yourself as a leader, you won't be able to make the hard decisions leaders sometimes need to make.[13]

Cookie Dough managers avoid conflict at all costs! Employees may take advantage of the soft approach of the Cookie Dough and, being soft and flexible, the manager may become ineffective.

The Rise to Leadership for Cookie Dough

For Cookie Dough to turn into a cookie when baking, a leavening agent such as baking powder is required. There is a difference,

---

13. Maxwell, John, The 21 Irrefutable Laws of Leadership: Follow Them and People Will Follow You, (Nashville, Tennessee, Thomas Nelson Inc., 2007)

then, between Cookie Dough designed to be Cookie Dough and Cookie Dough designed to be a cookie. When a manager begins his or her role in leadership, the expectation is that she or he will succeed as a leader. For true leadership to rise an ingredient is necessary. This ingredient is task behaviour. It is the Cookie Dough manager who is unable or unwilling to develop the ability to make tough decisions that becomes, almost counter-intuitively, a tough cookie.

The Struggle of Maury and the Missing Baking Powder

Maury was a nice guy. In fact, he was one of the nicest people one could have the good fortune of knowing. Maury was a logical choice for promotion. He cared about his colleagues, he showed appreciation to others, and he was keen to get started. I worked with Maury for the first two months of his new position. He worked very hard at applying sound leadership skills. He wanted to get it right. At the end of our coaching project, I was given feedback about Maury from his supervisor. It seemed that in all areas, Maury was doing very well. He had difficulty, however, holding a disciplinary conversation. He would get the hang of it, however, his supervisor relayed confidently.

I had the opportunity to speak with Maury about 12 months later. It seemed that Maury had gotten nicer. His supervisor was concerned, however, and asked me to speak with Maury. Maury's team's productivity was dropping. When it came to performance management, Maury was unwilling to intervene. He declared that there were reasons for each employee's decrease in performance and preferred to "cut them some slack." The employees, it seemed, appreciated this approach at first, but after a while came to expect it. Over time, the lack of addressing decreased performance resulted in a team with a very well-liked supervisor but little else.

I met with Maury. He was shocked that his performance as a supervisor was being called into question. He stated with great pride that any of his team members would do whatever he asked. He could not and would not treat them any other way. I discussed the balance of task and relationship behaviour. Admittedly, Maury had the relationship behaviour down pat. What was missing was Maury's understanding that having direct reports willing to do what was asked of them was great, but they needed to maintain performance independently. The relationships that Maury developed with his staff bordered on friendship, but being friends was counterproductive. The primary relationship needed to be one of supervisor and employee — equal but different, friendly but not friends.

The actions of collaborating, engaging, and problem-solving with an employee are the hallmarks of a good leader. I had a difficult time explaining how these excellent leadership qualities could be counterproductive. There were a few things happening, however, that I could point to such as:

1. Even though employees agreed to improve performance in one area, another area suffered.
2. The overall productivity of the team was dropping rapidly.
3. The atmosphere of the team, albeit friendly, became less focused on getting the work done and more focused on a casual approach to production.
4. Being a nice cookie earns as little respect as a Ginger snap snapping.

Sometimes you need to be more directive and less accommodating. Maury did not understand this. As stress increased, he was not able to "rise" to the occasion. He agreed to be more directive, but he made it clear to his team that he was following up on infractions more frequently only because the company said so. That message to his team was counterproductive. The situation devolved into an "us/them" approach. Maury and his team were on one side, and management was on the other. In the end, the company reassigned Maury to a less demanding position. They continued to support his development, as Maury had admitted that the demands of the job were overwhelming and impacted his judgement. He recognized, through coaching, that he preferred to avoid any situation that had the potential for conflict.

Directive Ain't Mean

Understanding that leadership means making tough decisions and adjusting the balance of task and relationship behaviours is key to effective supervision. Being both encouraging and directive are necessary elements for leading others. Being directive does not need to be punishing. I have personally experienced being held accountable without being punished.

In my first book, 5 Steps to Reducing Stress: Recognizing What Works, I acknowledged the work of my book coach, Les Kletke. It was true that I could not have started writing my book nor would I have finished it without his help. Les was encouraging, understanding, and supportive but (and yes, there is a but) he also held me accountable. I would joke that the stress of writing a chapter to meet a deadline was less stressful than having to explain to him why I did not meet the deadline! In a way, that statement was a joke, and in a way, it was true.

Holding me accountable consisted of reminding me of the goal. Someone didn't give up, and someone ensured I did not give up either. That someone was not me; it was my coach. Yes, he was there to help, but it was very clear I needed to do the work to obtain my goal. He had a great balance of task and relationship behaviour.

If You are Cookie Dough

I don't anticipate that after reading this chapter, leaders will stand up and exclaim to the world, "Hey, I'm Cookie Dough!" There are some things you can do, however, if you see any similarities between you and the description of cookie dough.

- When you hear the words "conflict" and "conflict resolution," what words come to mind? If you think or feel that conflict is a bad thing, you will be less willing to address a situation where there may be gaps in understanding. Additionally, conflict resolution may mean giving in, giving up, or an unnecessary conversation. If so, you might avoid conflict at all costs.
- Understand that your primary relationship at work is a professional one. Developing friendships, if not managed very carefully, lead to a perception of bias and complicate performance management conversations.
- Remember that allowing someone to do less of a job than is expected of her or him is not helpful in the long run. Your focus is to help develop an employee, and not solely focusing on making others feel good.
- Do you see yourself as a people pleaser? If so, and there is nothing negative about being one, determine if and when pleasing others gets in the way of needing to have a disciplinary conversation.
- If an employee agrees to increase productivity but does not, your approach is not working.
- Do not apologize for being a leader. Having authority is not negative; it is how you use authority that matters.

If You Work with or Know a Cookie Dough

Don't take advantage of this person by expecting he or she will always give you what you ask.

Ask yourself, "How am I contributing to this organization or am I using the goodwill of my leader to do less than I am able?"

Chapter 19 – Number 13 is a Monster

The Monster Cookie and the Riddle of a Baker's Dozen

Question: When does 13 really equal 12?
Answer: When it's a Baker's Dozen.

Question: When is a monster not a monster?
Answer: When it's a cookie.

Question: When is a tough cookie not a tough cookie?
Answer: When it's a Monster Cookie.

Confused? Read on.

It could be assumed, reasonably, that in a book about tough cookies, the Monster Cookie would be the meanest, most difficult, and toughest cookie of all. Nope, just the opposite. Refer to #3 above. "When is a tough cookie not a tough cookie?" The answer is, "When it's a Monster Cookie." A Monster Cookie represents a tough cookie that has understood how to improve his or her interpersonal skills and has taken action to make it happen.

There is no perfect formula for becoming a Monster Cookie. Just like growth—the path of development for tough cookies is unique. No two tough cookie humans will be alike in their development.

The Canadian Smartie

In Canada, we add Smarties to our Monster Cookies. Smarties come in a small box filled with multi-coloured, candy-covered chocolate. Considering all the ingredients that could be in a Monster Cookie, the Smartie is the ingredient of choice for our Monster Cookies. The analogy of a leader becoming "smart" about their need to develop from a tough cookie to Monster Cookie is a good one. The Smartie represents the pieces of knowledge, wisdom, and ability the person must add to cease being a tough cookie. Some Monster Cookies have more Smarties than others.

Some tough cookies adjust their behaviours more easily. Some tough cookies become Monster Cookies only briefly. When the going gets tough, they revert to their tough cookie behaviours.

In conclusion, the Monster Cookie is not scary – it's a good thing. You want to be a Monster Cookie, and you want a workforce made up of monsters—well, Monster Cookies.

Before It's Too Late

I like to think I'm a monster—I mean a Monster Cookie. I believe I have realized and implemented the behaviours required for me to shift from a Sugar Cookie to a Monster Cookie. True, when people asked me what I wanted to be when I grew up, "I want to become a Monster Cookie" wasn't one of my answers. Perhaps for my parents, I had already earned the right to be called a monster— but I digress. As a Sugar Cookie, I am aware when the (my) sugar starts heating beyond usefulness or reason. As an extrovert, my feelings are on the surface. People who know me can tell when I am angry even when I believe I'm not showing it. Those who don't know me very well see mostly the sugar. Those who work with me see the Monster Cookie. If I am in a new and very stressful situation, however, the sugar starts to bubble. I lose my Monster Cookie status and like a very cheesy horror flick, I turn from Monster Cookie to tough Sugar Cookie. Now that's scary! In my previous book, 5 Steps to Reducing Stress: Recognizing What Works, I relayed my need to find quick and easy ways to reduce stress. The impetus for change and the need to do it quickly came from knowing that when my sugar is burnt, there is no going back. I become a burnt friend, family member, colleague, etc. Consequently, the need for stress-reducing strategies to reduce the heat, avoid the burn, and remain a Monster Cookie.

The process of losing my Monster Cookie status looks something like the following:

1. I am exposed to something that is shocking. It has to have a big impact. It needs to be the type of shock that goes against something very important. Perhaps something that I believed to be true and found out otherwise. It needs to be something that goes against my core values.

2. I will use logic to find a way to explain what has happened. I might even ignore the situation as a "one-off" event.

3. It happens again.

4. I react. I get to the point very, very fast! "I can't believe you just said that!" I exclaimed (loudly) to an acquaintance. As a Monster Cookie I could have brought the situation to his attention in a much different way. The person was shocked that I a) used that tone of voice, and b) used that tone of voice with him. The conversation deteriorated, slightly. I felt the burn of the sugar and backed off. Using some instant stress-reducing techniques, I implemented damage control, and we carried on, Monster Cookie intact.

5. It happens again, only worse.

6. The sugar heats faster than before. It starts to become unmanageable. It starts to burn. My comments become sharper, my insights become piercing (and not in a good way), and I become more and more rigid. Interestingly enough, while I am still protesting, I am not fully burnt.

7. It happens again.

8. I'm burnt. There may be one last-ditch effort to straighten the situation out but probably not. As a burnt Sugar Cookie, I withdraw completely. There is no "un-burning" the sugar. That is it. I am done. I am not just being stubborn; something inside me shuts down and shuts. The burning hurts, it is upsetting, and it is stressful. I will suffer physically by being drained, psychologically by being confused about what happened and why, and emotionally by being sad, replicating a grieving process about what has been lost.

9. I may, once again, look like a Monster Cookie in that situation or with that person. Upon closer examination, however, he would feel that something is missing, something is different. I may revert to being a Monster Cookie, but a few Smarties are missing. There are burnt sugar pieces in their places.

The burnt sugar incident as described above happens rarely. It takes a lot to get to that point. In almost all other situations, I can feel the burn, implement the stress management strategies that work for me, and I am back in the land of Monster Cookies. I don't want to be the burnt sugar, but it is in me to be a tough cookie.

Learning to be a Monster Cookie

All tough cookies can become monster cookies. First you need to recognize you are a tough cookie and what type you are. Each of us who recognizes our tough cookie traits needs to allow the Monster Cookie to develop. We do this by building our soft skills, specifically those related to our cookie type. We do this by feeding it with logical thought and positive intentions, listening for understanding, giving effective feedback and many, many other strong interpersonal skills. If you would like more detail on the topic of interpersonal skills, I would suggest reading In a Perfect World by Pat Hirst.[14]

Maintaining Monster Cookie status is not easy. Recognize the early warning signs of forthcoming trouble. Note them, put them on an index card, and place it in your pocket to read throughout the day. Do what you need to do to remember the early warning signs of your tough cookie traits and have a strategy to deal with them so that you may return to being a Monster Cookie.

Once you have developed the skills and are more of a Monster Cookie than a tough cookie, you will notice something happening to your interactions with others. They get much smoother. As a

---

14. Pat Hirst, In a Perfect World: Interpersonal Skills for Life (Victoria: FriesenPress, 2015).

tough cookie, you have traits that have worked for you in the past, but they will no longer work for you in the present and definitely won't work for others around you. Once you have the knowledge and the skills to be a Monster Cookie, reverting to your previous tough cookie traits will not serve you well. Those around you will react with more intensity to the negative behaviours' returning than they did when the behaviours were present on a regular basis. When this happens, you will have a lot of crumbs to clean up!

Developing into a Monster Cookie is not easy. At first, it will seem to go against your nature. Develop and grow by modifying your behaviour as a tough cookie. Recognize what is working and what not working. When difficult and stressful times arise, have a strategy ready to reduce the stress and allow your advanced skills to gain control once again.

Chapter 20: Inside the Cookie Jar: Cookie Interactions

Ode to the Baker's Dozen

Whether Black and White or Ginger Snap,
Fortune-telling or looking back,
to see the Hermit Cookie disappear
from all complaints, it cannot hear.
The Oatmeal Raisin doesn't mind
the absence since it is, in kind,
the type that doesn't want to change
much to the chagrin of those engaged
in moving forward with the new,
led by the Imperial Cookie, who
has more talk than walk and with lots of fluff
tries to act like a Chocolate Puff.
The Double Chocolate Chip Macadamia Nut
insults the Sugar Cookie but
the Cookie Dough is there to make
Refrigerator Cookies take
the time to stabilize themselves
when hearing what the Shortbread tells

the others of the need to be
the best, the fastest, the tastiest indeed.
Otherwise, the company fails
to do the job that entails
all the cookies do their best
to get along with all the rest.
Only one can do that now—
the Monster Cookie, which has figured out how
to make things work and make things flow,
from Ginger Snap to Cookie Dough.

The Reality of Tough Cookies' Working Together

Some people get along. Some people don't. There are differences that cause tension and conflict between and among people. Someone who is very outgoing, for example, may overwhelm someone who is not. Someone who likes to get to the bottom line may frustrate those who prefer more detail and context in a conversation. Many personality profiles detail differences in how we like to communicate, deal with conflict, see the world, and express our talents. It is the same within the world of cookies. Some cookies conflict more with one type than with the others.

In the preceding chapters, you have read descriptions of tough cookies. You have probably identified others' fitting into the types or, hopefully, you have identified your own type. One type is not any better or worse than another.

Regardless, cookies need to get along. If you can identify the traits of tough cookie friends, family members, or colleagues, you have a better chance of accommodating their behaviours. You have a better chance of getting along because you can understand tough cookies a little more comprehensively.

Some of the more common conflicts are depicted in the following diagrams:

Ginger Snap

- Frustrates Black and White by not following rules
- Oatmeal Raisin feels pressured. Becomes more resistant as a result.
- The Cookie Dough finds the snapping offensive
- The Hermit doesn't understand what all the fuss is about.
- The Sugar Cookie finds the snapping hurtful
- Refrigerater Cookie freezes
- Fortune Cookie takes snapping as evidence that things are going from bad to worse.

.1

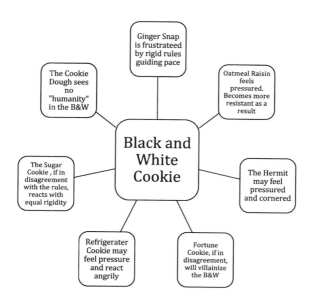

Black and White Cookie

- Ginger Snap is frustrateed by rigid rules guiding pace
- Oatmeal Raisin feels pressured. Becomes more resistant as a result
- The Cookie Dough sees no "humanity" in the B&W
- The Hermit may feel pressured and cornered
- The Sugar Cookie , if in disagreement with the rules, reacts with equal rigidity
- Refrigerater Cookie may feel pressure and react angrily
- Fortune Cookie, if in disagreement, will villainize the B&W

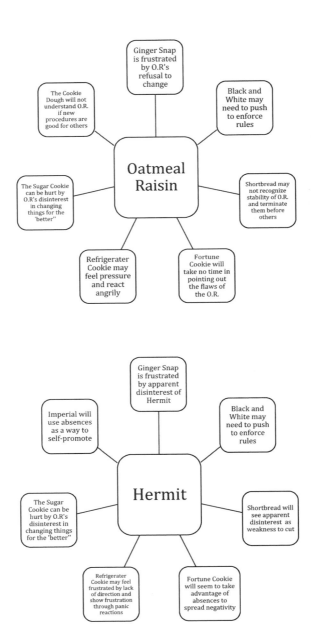

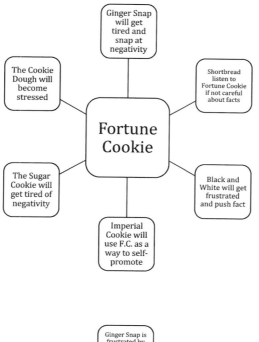

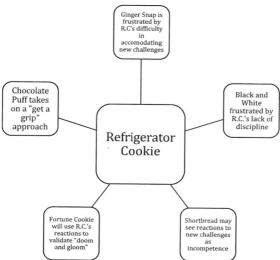

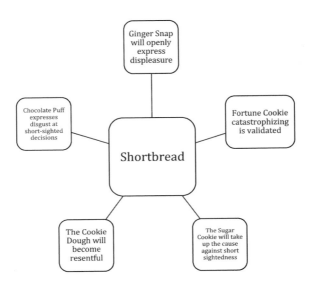

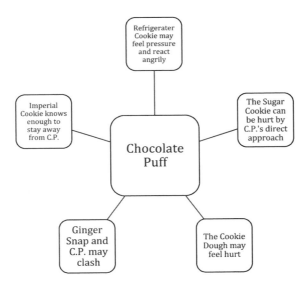

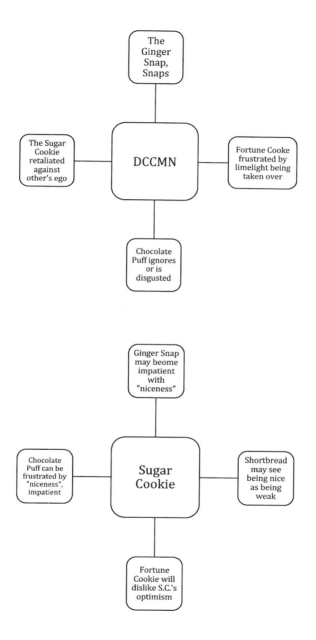

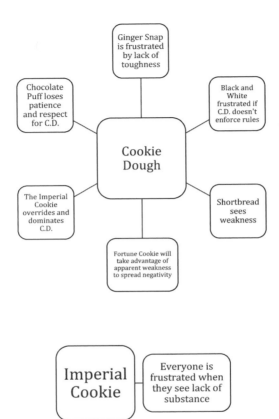

Creating a Cookie Team. What's it Gonna Take?

I was asked to hold a team-building session with six managers. The company wanted the managers to improve their communication with each other and work as a team rather than a collection of individuals. The managers needed to support each other. Being divided and demonstrating doubt, or worse, a lack of respect for each other was impacting their direct reports. This resulted in the formation of a series of "us and them" camps. This was not good for productivity. The managers needed to put aside their interpersonal difficulties, work through them, or at least agree to disagree in the best interest of the organization.

I planned a group session; it was a must attend (otherwise the Hermit Cookie might not have shown). I needed the supervisors to understand the importance of teamwork. It requires each member to endorse the approach, accommodate each other's perspectives, and use flexibility to deal with differing opinions.

I led the group through a series of questions and exercises designed to a) demonstrate the importance of teamwork, b) help them build a strategy to get there, and c) do so by utilizing their cookie types. The exercises allowed the supervisors to interact, discuss each other's perspectives on teams, develop a team strategy on how to work together more effectively, and to understand the strengths and challenges of each supervisor.

The cookie profile was as follows:

1. One Black and White Cookie
2. One Oatmeal Raisin Cookie
3. One Hermit Cookie
4. One Ginger Snap
5. One Chocolate Puff
6. Once Cookie Dough

The strategies I used were as follows:

1. Show why teamwork is necessary.
   a. The Black and White Cookie needs facts

   I presented research, statistics, case studies and examples of how teams operate and operate more efficiently than individuals.

   b. The Oatmeal Raisin needs evidence

The team completed a task as an individual then as a team. They were able to complete the task better and faster as a team.

c. The Hermit Cookie needs to realize that all members are required for a team to work.

The team completed another exercise demonstrating how one person on a team can prevent positive results.

d. The Chocolate Puff and the Ginger Snap will tolerate the exercises if you don't drag this out.

e. The Cookie Dough is good to go!

2. Start planning. I asked the team to analyze the opportunities and barriers to becoming a team.

a. The Chocolate Puff needs to know that being a team is being strong. I defined collaboration as being cooperative and assertive showing that teamwork doesn't mean you have to agree, let your guard down, or end the day in a group hug

b. The Oatmeal Raisin needs validation of current strategies.

I presented teamwork as something that is already in existence within the team but needs tweaking. Planning for a complete overhaul of their interaction would shut down the Oatmeal Raisin Cookie. You will then need to deal with the dried-up oatmeal. It would be easier to shift cement.

c. The Ginger Snap needs to participate in collaboration. The other cookies need to show they are not intimidated.

We discussed why it is important to check things out with the other managers before acting on impulse and emotion.

d. The Cookie Dough needs to be assertive.

I asked the Cookie Dough to lead the discussion about how managers would support each other.

Chapter 21: The Report Card

I have been fortunate enough to work with many tough cookies over the years. As noted, most tough cookies have good intentions but how they come across to others has not worked well. Good intentions are a good start. They are not, however, enough. Remember where the road went that was paved with good intentions.

Within one three-month period, I worked with five tough cookies. I had one hour, twice a month for three months available to coach each of the five managers. Six hours was not enough time to shift the managers' behaviours. It was, however, a start. Out of the five managers, three were newly promoted; one had been in the position for three years, while the fifth had served as a manager for 22 years. Their profiles were as follows:

1. Newly promoted Cookie Dough
2. Newly promoted Ginger Snap
3. Newly promoted Refrigerator Cookie
4. The 3-year manager was a Hermit Cookie
5. The 22-year manager was just tired

The Cookie Dough Report

The newly promoted Cookie Dough was very eager to learn how to be an effective manager. We worked on implementing the five characteristics of an exemplary leader (see Kouzes and Posner's The Leadership Challenge). One practice, called "Encourage the Heart," ensures that the manager knows how essential is recognizing and showing appreciation for direct reports' efforts. The manager needs to encourage others—frequently, sincerely, and by attaching encouragement to positive behaviour. This newly promoted manager excelled at making others feel positive and valued. He showed all the promise of being one of the best supervisors for that position. Unfortunately, as his job became increasingly demanding and stressful, he defaulted to being a leader who only encouraged the heart. He was unable to hold disciplinary conversations. The more pressure he felt to address poor performance, the more stressed he became. The more stressed he became, the more he focused on relationships and not the tasks that needed to be completed. He was willing but not able to demonstrate behaviours required for him to effectively manage performance. His report card as a manager would look something like the following:

Cookie Dough Report Card

Willingness to learn	A+	
Ability when things run smoothly	B+	*A new manager, but with potential.*
Willingness to change behaviour	C	*Did not see the value of a disciplinary conversation. Preferred to ask employee to perform better.*
Ability to change behaviour under stress	D	*Might execute a disciplinary conversation if pressed but would ensure the employee knew it was because he had no choice.*

Cookie Dough Report Card

Work Left to Do

6. Needs to understand the helpfulness of correcting an employee's performance.
7. Practice coaching conversations.
8. Understand the difference between being assertive, aggressive, and submissive.

Homework:

Answer the following questions:

1. What is the difference between discipline and punishment?
2. How would a coaching conversation help a direct report develop?
3. What is the difference between a coaching conversation and a disciplinary conversation? When do you use each one with a direct report?
4. What does "writing up" an employee mean to you?

Action to Take:

1. Survey with a 360-degree leadership Development Inventory

The Ginger Snap Report

The Ginger Snap was willing to learn new behaviours. He saw the value of increasing his relations with others. As a result, he worked hard at turning his reaction into a response. He had difficulty transferring his learning, however, to new and challenging situations. His snap returned under stress.

Ginger Snap Report Card

Willingness to learn	A	
Ability when things run smoothly	A	*Was able to spend time on building relationships while guiding the tasks of the team.*

Ginger Snap Report Card

Willingness to change behaviour	A	He understood the change was necessary.
Ability to change behaviour under stress	D – F	The Ginger Snap excelled in the arena in which he applied his newly acquired knowledge and behaviours. He defaulted to previous "snapping" in other situations:

- He snapped when talking with colleagues who did not share the same perspective on work situations.
- He snapped when challenged on a decision he made with his team.
- Snapping was done less in person and more through email.
- Since people around him were not used to him losing his temper, his reacting angrily (even if it was less of a display than before) was surprising and seemed extreme. "Oh no! Here we go again!" was a common concern.

Work Left to Do

1. Understand that extreme "snapping" is not acceptable in the workplace nor is it helpful in any relationship.
2. Increase impulse control, especially under stress.
3. Recognize behaviour under stress.
4. Understand that controlling a situation does not mean dominating a situation.
5. Understand the difference between being assertive, aggressive and submissive

Ginger Snap Report Card

Homework:

Answer the following questions:
1. How does punishment differ from discipline?
2. What are the consequences of punishment?
3. What behaviours do you demonstrate that others might consider punishing?
4. What actions do you need to take to mute your reaction and respond more appropriately in a difficult situation?

Action to Take:

1. Complete emotional intelligence 360-degree feedback, paying close attention to impulse control.
2. Work on managing stress by identifying triggering situations and the signals of becoming frustrated and angry before exploding.
3. Use stress management techniques to counteract the stress response.
4. Identify the underlying beliefs and judgements you hold about other people.

The Refrigerator Cookie Report

The Refrigerator Cookie was impressive. She was a bit apprehensive about "being coached" but warmed to the idea when she realized it might help her as a new manager. She was efficient, technically proficient, a steady and hard worker, and had a desire to achieve … perfection. Enter the unstable ingredient of perfectionism.

When she was faced with new tasks and new responsibilities with an emphasis on multi-tasking, it caused her great stress. As a result, the unstable ingredient of perfectionism caused her to "melt down." She needed to change her behaviour and she did.

Refrigerator Cookie Report Card

Willingness to learn	B – A	At first, but when she realized it would be helpful and not critical, A.
Ability when things run smoothly	A	
Willingness to change behaviour	A+	Once committed to the process, she studied and learned how to modify her behaviour
Ability to change behaviour under stress	A	Once she knew what to do, she practised, analyzed, and practised some more.

Work Left to Do

To recognize warning signs of melt down and practice selected stress management strategies

Homework:

Answer the following questions:
1. What happens to you emotionally, behaviourally, physically, and cognitively when you start to feel distressed?
2. What are your go-to strategies in these situations?

Action to Take:

1. Monitor your stress level, implement strategies, evaluate, modify strategies, and continue.

The Hermit Cookie Report

Three years as a manager and the Hermit Cookie was becoming increasingly hermit-like. Our coaching sessions were not different. The manager stated that he was supportive of the coaching, but his resolve was not apparent in his behaviour. In our coaching sessions, he frequently took calls, was late for appointments, and did not complete homework assignments. Even though I brought these behaviours to his attention, he apologized, but did not change.

Hermit Report Card

Willingness to learn	B	At first, indicated he was willing to do what he needed to improve his supervisory behaviours.
Ability when things run smoothly	C	He did not communicate well with his direct reports or the other managers, and he needed to.
Willingness to change behaviour	D	There was little indication that he was willing since he did not complete any of the tasks he was assigned.
Ability to change behaviour under stress	D – F	With increasing pressure, the manager became increasingly distant.

Work Left to Do

1. Little could be done without the willingness of the manager.

Homework:

1. To practice management-by-walking-around and checking in with his direct reports.
2. To provide unsolicited help to the employees.
3. Engage employees by asking them how he, as their supervisor, can help.
4. Listen to new ideas, seek them out and encourage employees to share their thoughts and ideas.

The Tired Manager

This manager might have been referred to as an Oatmeal Raisin, but this manager wasn't a tough cookie as much as he was someone who was tired of his job. He showed up each day and did a good job, but he tended not to follow through, sometimes, on new procedures. He communicated pleasantly but with little to no enthusiasm. His ability was not in question. His willingness was also not in question. He was able to recognize how much he wanted to retire. Shortly after, he did.

The Impact of Commitment

Identifying one's own negative behaviour is hopeful, but achieving results takes not only self-awareness but also real commitment to the following:

1. To look for specific behaviours that are problematic for others
2. To be willing to change behaviours by practicing them and overlearning them
3. To examine the underlying beliefs that facilitate the less desirable behaviours
4. To adopt specific strategies that must be practiced and executed when necessary
5. To be willing to be coached to change behaviours
6. To take the time to listen, ask questions, take notes, and otherwise show a genuine interest in the coaching process
7. To celebrate small changes and big wins
8. To allow yourself the mistakes of reverting to previous behaviour but ensure you execute both damage control and return to new learned behaviour
9. To seek feedback often from others about your improvement, if any
10. To be aware that the old ways of being do not serve you
11. To practice, evaluate, adjust, practice, evaluate, adjust—forever
12. To not allow habit to return you to a state of "toughness"
13. To take setbacks as opportunities to adjust your learning
14. To take on the challenge of changing behaviour but not your personality
15. To breathe and move forward with responses, not reactions

16. To remember, you might not be right

Answering and addressing these statements will help you adjust your tough cookie status. Remember, it is not about being right or being wrong. It is about being collaborative when required.

Chapter 22: Help! I Have Tough Cookies on My Team.

Organizations make the error of promoting someone to a managerial position simply because they excel in their current position. The assumption is success in one equates to success in the other. This is not true. Unfortunately, organizations tend to be slow learners. Consider the following sequence of events:

- Great potential in this employee. She does great work. Let's promote her!
- Okay, she's new, she's learning, she's pleased to be recognized, and she's starting out well.
- Oops, that was a mistake on her part. Maybe just a misstep. She's new.
- Oh, wow, that's interesting. She doesn't seem to be connecting well with her team. She's new.
- Oh, my. That's not so good. Her team is getting quite discouraged. Let's intervene. Let's talk. She's new ... but ...
- Well, our talk didn't seem to do much. It helped for a while, but it didn't last. Since she is no longer new, some

significant intervention is required. Let's get her a coach. After all, we are all about development.

- Ah, she is doing much better; it's been a couple of months now. Coaching seems to be successful. Coaching is finished since she's doing so well. Whew!
- What has happened? It seemed to be going so well! Now it's been three months since her last coaching session. More coaching is needed.
- That is better. It's been six months, now. Her behaviour is better and seems stable. Her coach has worked with her team to ensure they know what to expect (and require) from each other.
- Yikes! Another misstep with a team member and another with a colleague. Wait, she's handling it. Crisis averted. This just might work.
- It's working; it's been 2 years.
- "Great potential in this employee, let's promote him..."

What Can I Expect in Tough Cookie Development?

Tough cookies need to change behaviour. This may sound simple but it's not easy. A true change in behaviour occurs only through learning and subsequent development. Learning requires a shift in behaviour, maintained by internal motivation and development. Let's look at the path taken by a tough cookie from behavioural change through to learning and development. Consider the following.

Situation:

The tough cookie receives information about what behaviours need to be changed ...

Behavioural change:

a. The tough cookie makes the changes but does not apply them to different situations or over time.
b. The tough cookie has not learned.
c. Learning:
d. The tough cookie wants to make the changes, understands the need for them and looks for ways to improve. She is internally motivated.
e. The tough cookie uses both trial and error and information to modify behaviour in a variety of situations.
f. The tough cookie is learning.
g. Development
h. The tough cookie stumbles but uses what she has learned to correct behaviour.
i. The tough cookie applies these changes over time and across situations on a regular basis.
j. The desired behaviours are maintained.
k. The tough cookie has developed.
l. There is a reasonably predictable timeline with most tough cookies who are learning and developing.

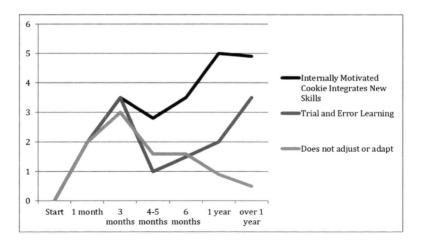

New managers face a steep learning curve. They have to learn the technical aspects of the job and the interpersonal ones as well. It takes about three months for a person to attain a degree of technical proficiency. During this time, co-workers are generally quite forgiving. Interpersonal errors can be made, and there are no serious repercussions. With time, however, interpersonal relations become more important. If the manager is unable to adjust or adapt using soft skills, forgiveness gives way to fear, distrust, frustration, or rumours of incompetence.

Manager development tends to follow one of three tracks:

1. The manager is unable to adapt. Interpersonal tension increases. The manager's behaviour becomes more erratic in an effort to solve the problem. This results in further alienation and validates the employees' poor opinions of the manager. When performance drops and complaints increase, the organization steps in with feedback, coaching, and training. It may help at first, but the progress is not maintained, and the manager reverts to previous behaviours. The manager may be willing but unable to modify the behaviour. The manager may be able but not willing to modify the behaviour. Either way, it's a dead-end road for this manager's career as a supervisor.

2. The manager learns by trial and error. In this path, the manager benefits from feedback, coaching, and training. Navigating the human aspects of the job is difficult but not impossible. The demands of needing to adjust and adapt her own style to the situation become overwhelming. The manager reverts to previous behaviours then realizes her mistakes. The damage is done, and with relationships, the manager has taken one step forward but two steps back. The good news is that many managers who learn by trial and error eventually learn the skills they need and go on to

be successful leaders, though there is significant collateral damage along the way.

3. The manager integrates new information. The manager who understands and accepts the fact that relationship-oriented behaviours are essential may make errors, but the negative impact is short-term. This manager will do whatever it takes to improve his soft skills and learn to apply them to the right degree and in the right circumstance. This manager has moved from being a tough cookie to a Monster Cookie!

Knowing what types of cookies you supervise allows you to understand your employees' strengths and challenges. Knowing this allows you to be an effective manager for each type. For example, you would not expect a Black and White Cookie to understand that policies are guidelines and sometimes you have to go beyond "doing things right" to "doing the right thing." Your understanding allows you to spend more time coaching the Black and White Cookie in this area. You will have an answer to the question you will inevitably have: "What in the world was he thinking?"

Chapter 23: Cleaning up the Crumbs

This book reflects what I have observed over years of coaching tough cookies. I noticed patterns of behaviours and called them cookies. When we discover ways to describe patterns of behaviours by giving them names or labels, we run the risk of stereotyping others. This is one thing we must not do. Albeit the patterns were created from observations and grouped into categories, nothing can account for nor explain the whole self. One's motivation and intent are hidden; they are internal. As a result, we have no direct knowledge about why a person behaves as he does. That knowledge can only be shared through open and respectful dialogue.

What is the difference between identifying traits in a person or in a group of people and stereotyping? Identifying traits helps us understand a person. It opens up communication by giving us a "language" the other prefers and increases the potential of our being empathic. We acknowledge that the trait does not describe the whole person. Many of us stereotype, unfortunately, when we learn about any type, style or trait placing people into categories.

Stereotyping limits our understanding of one another. We take one trait and use it to explain everything about the other person or persons. Stereotyping is negative. It uses traits such as race, gender, and hair colour, to explain things such as performance, and intelligence. Understand cookies. Don't stereotype them.

Some cookies only become tough cookies when they are stressed. And some cookies are tougher than others. A person can show up as a tough cookie in one circumstance and not in another. When working with a tough cookie, check your assumptions about their intentions. Focus on and have dialogue about behaviour, not about the person. When we remove the judgement that tough cookies are awful people, we get to where we need to be, which is ... on better terms with them. In doing so, we may help tough cookies behave in ways that are a little less tough and encourage them to be effective monster managers.

The Impact

It's not enough to be self-aware. It's not enough to recognize another's tough cookie traits; you need to see the strengths from which those traits develop. You need to be able to not only notice yourself, but also the strength of others, and most importantly your impact on them. Be aware of the impact of your words, your actions, and your beliefs. If you believe that a Cookie Dough is only weak or too nice, this is all that you will see. What you see, therefore, validates your poor opinion of the Cookie Dough.

In order to work as a team, cookies and even cookies in conflict, must park their egos at the proverbial company door and keep the best interests of the company in mind. Understanding the other cookies in the cookie jar as well as being aware of potential tough cookie clashes, allows tough cookies to work together without creating a lot of conflict—a lot of crumbs.

About the Author

Genella Macintyre has been a trainer, coach, and consultant for over 25 years. She is president of Partners in Discovery Ltd., a coaching, training, and consulting business that she founded in 1993, where she works as an international trainer and leadership consultant. Genella was Executive Director of the Shilo Military Family Resource Centre from 1993 to 2003, and has also served as a  counselor for military and civilian families alike. She has taught at both the University of Manitoba and the University of Winnipeg (where she still teaches) and has been a trainer with the Province of Manitoba for the past 17 years.

Genella holds a master's degree in Applied Social Psychology, is a Certified Psychological Health and Safety Advisor, is a Certified John Maxwell Group Team Member, and is also a certified EQi2.0 (Emotional Intelligence) Trainer. In addition, she holds certifications in Myers-Briggs Type Inventory, The Enneagram, Strength Deployment Inventory, Mediation Skills, Harassment Investigations, and Resolution Training.